NATASHA'S STORY

MICHAEL NICHOLSON

NATASHA'S STORY

M

MACMILLAN

LONDON

First published 1993 by Macmillan London
a division of Pan Macmillan Publishers Limited
Cavaye Place London SW10 9PG
and Basingstoke
Associated companies throughout the world

ISBN 0 333 59574 2

1 3 5 7 9 8 6 4 2

A CIP catalogue record for this book is available from
the British Library

Phototypeset by Intype, London

Printed and bound in Great Britain by
Mackays of Chatham PLC, Chatham, Kent

THIS BOOK IS DEDICATED
TO
NATASHA
AND ALL THOSE SHE LEFT BEHIND

ACKNOWLEDGEMENTS

Much of Natasha's story is personal, therefore a little of it must be left untold. Nothing of substance is lost, that I promise.

Much of Bosnia's story is also my own account as a reporter and witness. But some of it is not and I am indebted to the corps of honourable British correspondents and colleagues who for month after month braved the rigours and horrors of the Bosnian war to report it. Their dispatches helped me fill in the gaps and I salute them . . . Robert Fox, Patrick Bishop, Marcus Tanner, Martin Bell, Tony Birtley, Ed Vulliamy, Maggie O'Kane, David Williams, John Sweeney and others.

My special gratitude to Michael Montgomery, who first introduced me to Ljubica Ivezic orphanage. My thanks to Dr Mark Wheeler of London University's School of Slavonic and East European Studies, for his help with the historical background, to Felicity Rubinstein for first suggesting the book and to ITN for giving me the space to write it.

Finally and as ever, my thanks to Diana who, after twenty-five years, must have thought the worst was over!

LIST OF ILLUSTRATIONS

'They have taken her away and I am left with the halfwit. He stands in the corner of the room, half in light, one eye closed, the other wide and unblinking, half a smile, half a scowl, brave for an instant, moving into the lamp's glare, then scurrying back into his corner, hiding from me and all the misery surrounding us.

The window is criss-crossed with sticky tape, and I can see the hills surrounding Sarajevo. Across the scorched and blackened tiled rooftops of the old quarter are the forests where the Serbs are dug in with their guns, the guns that have shattered this city and all but silenced its people.

They hit this orphanage a week ago and blew a hole in the side of the nursery, which is why the children are sheltering in the cellar. Natasha is there now.

On the far side of the city, smoke is rising as straight and as black as a chimney. Something is always burning here and someone always dying. Maybe a Serb sniper is there even now, training his sights on this window, seeing my shadow in the light. I can imagine a mortar being pushed through the mud somewhere inside the cover of those trees and soon there will be another flash and a thousand searing fragments and another bout of dying. This is a city waiting to die and the world is watching. And here I sit, a stranger in Sarajevo, come to take away a little orphan girl.

They come back and she is with them, holding their hands tightly, not looking at me. Yes, they say smiling, she will come with you to England but she asks how long she will stay. You understand? She wants to know how much love she must give.

I hear the familiar rumble outside, flashes of light in the darkening sky, the beginning of the night's bombardment. Someone brings in coffee, I break open a bar of chocolate. Then they tell me Natasha's story.'

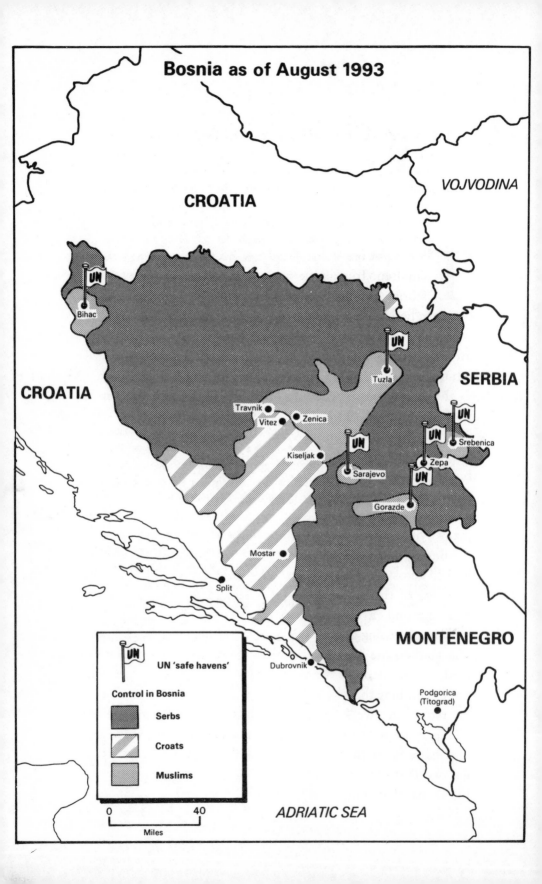

Bosnia as of August 1993

CROATIA

VOJVODINA

Bihac

CROATIA

Tuzla

SERBIA

Travnik
Zenica
Vitez
Srebenica
Kiseljak
Zepa
Sarajevo
Gorazde

Split
Mostar

MONTENEGRO

Dubrovnik

Podgorica
(Titograd)

UN 'safe havens'

Control in Bosnia

Serbs

Croats

Muslims

ADRIATIC SEA

0   40

Miles

CHAPTER ONE

This is not one tale but two: of Bosnia and of one of her children. To read the one you must read the other; their stories are interwoven, their fates entwined. Natasha's begins in besieged Sarajevo and ends in England. Bosnia's starts with Independence and finishes in bloody oblivion. Here, then, are two stories of a land that died and of a child that was reborn.

I first saw Bosnia from across the River Drina in Serbia. It was the summer of '91, the Serbs had begun their war on Croatia and the killing fields were already staining red the old map of Yugoslavia. I was not new to the destruction business but the ferocity of the Serb battalions as they swept across the country startled me as it shocked every correspondent who came to cover that war. Such devastation, such brutality, so many dying.

But on that warm day in late summer, how peaceful Bosnia looked across the Drina. We crossed an old stone toll bridge at the edge of the rolling fields of wheat to the small medieval town beyond, a tall spired church, the dome of an ancient mosque glistening gold in the sun, the cobbled streets, the bustling market, the horse and donkey carts, the old men playing cards in the shade of the chestnut trees. Thank God, we said, there is nothing the Serbs want here.

How little we knew then of Bosnia or the Serbs. What strangers we were to the Balkans and the simmering ambitions and hatreds so thinly disguised there. How could we have guessed that day, as we sipped Turkish coffee on the banks of the Drina, that soon those same Serb battalions would cross it and tear this beautiful land and its people to pieces? The land that to all the world had meant harmony, tolerance and peace.

What did we know then of the Bosnians? Were they one nation or three? What besides the hypen did the Serb-, Croat- and Muslim-Bosnian have in common? What kept them together? And what was it, on that fateful April day last year, that dashed Natasha's country to pieces for ever?

It was a Friday in July and, given what we were doing and where we were going, it was just as well that it was not the thirteenth. Flying at 20,000 feet, the pilot told us we were safely above missile height, which was cold comfort. What all of us were dreading most was the landing. We were on our way to Sarajevo in an RAF Hercules, affectionately known to their crews as 'Fat Alberts'. This was the first United Nations relief flight to attempt to land in that city since it had come under siege three months before. Trussed up in nets were pallets of powdered baby milk, disposable nappies, sterilized water for the hospitals and 3000 packets of ready-to-eat military rations. A flight that ought normally to take twenty minutes would take four times as long because the pilot was edging around known and potentially hostile Serbian anti-aircraft batteries. His last radio message said the airport was safe but we wondered just how safe that was. What were our chances if some cussed rogue Serb gunner on the hills overlooking the runway suddenly decided to make it unsafe as our wheels touched tarmac, when we were at our most vulnerable, the easiest, fattest rolling target?

It is not considered brave to think such things but it is hard to be anything but cowardly when you are so entirely dependent on one man's skill and another's deadly intentions. A red light blinked above me and the loadmaster held up five fingers, five minutes to landing. I looked out of the tiny window to bright, clear Bosnia below and remembered how earnestly we had been praying for cloud to cover our approach. The light flashed red again and the soldiers around me strapped on their bullet-proof flak-jackets, tightened their harnesses and laid their rifles across their knees. Then we banked sharply and the little courage I had left drained away as we began our steep descent into the valley of Sarajevo.

Until that moment, Vukovar and Osjiek had been my own two experiences of the war that was splitting Yugoslavia into so many pieces. Both had been large, prosperous towns in eastern Croatia until the Serbian-dominated federal army attacked and destroyed them under the pretence of maintaining Yugoslavia's integrity. At Osjiek, I had nearly been killed when a rocket hit my hotel, demolishing room 386 as I sat on my bed three rooms along the corridor at 389. The day before, I was in a helicopter carrying the Dutch Ambassador and two Serbian generals when Croatian bullets came in one side and out the other, tearing open the port fuel tank and forcing the pilot to make an emergency landing. Had the helicopter been hit by red-hot tracer rounds, it would have exploded.

Until Sarajevo, Vukovar was the deadliest and saddest story of all. It had been a pretty, bustling market town on the banks of the Danube – many a British tourist will have postcards of it tucked away somewhere in a holiday album. Much of it was medieval, with narrow winding streets and lanes of tiny cob cottages, and tall, beautiful spires – more churches, I think, than I had ever seen in any one place. But Vukovar committed suicide.

One August evening two years ago, a column of federal tanks came rumbling to the outskirts of the town, their gun barrels aimed at the centre. Without delay, their commander sent his runner with an ultimatum: surrender or be destroyed. The good people of Vukovar chose to ignore him. Perhaps they thought it inconceivable that an army which had for so long been their guardian could now be their assassin. The commander was not a patient man – his orders forbade him that luxury – so he did not wait to give them a second chance. From that night on, his tanks, and the howitzers that followed them, pounded the town without interruption. When September came, nothing lived long that did not live underground. By

October, the winds that brought the rains and the bitter cold carried to those of us witnessing and reporting the destruction from the outside, the awful stench of the dead and, in the rare moments of stillness, when the guns were quiet, the dreadful cries of the living.

Then, on 16 November, it was over. After ninety-seven days and nights of bombardment like no other in Europe since 1945, Vukovar, the symbol of Croatian defiance, fell. That same afternoon, at an agreed rendezvous and with the International Red Cross as guarantors of safe passage, the survivors surrendered themselves. Slowly, hesitantly, they came shuffling towards us, out from behind the barricades, a long, winding, tragic human convoy, many of them limping without shoes, on a road littered with shrapnel, shivering without clothes in the icy drizzle, women and girls, grown men and children, young men and old all quietly weeping. Most of them were seeing daylight for the first time in months, having survived in cellars and sewers; they had only heard and guessed at the death and devastation above. The town behind them was still burning but nobody cared. Occasional gunfire still sounded but nobody listened. The survivors in Vukovar passed the dead in the streets without a glance, so used to death were they, the stiff and bloated dead, some burned black like grotesque sticks of charcoal, others naked, stripped of clothes by their killers.

The hospital morgue had overflowed into the orchards nearby and hundreds of bodies lay beneath the torn stumps of apple trees in neat, orderly lines, bleached faces under wet grey sheets, a number inked on their foreheads, mother, child, soldier, farmer, innocents and combatants side by side. There were more dead than I had ever seen together before, more than we could decently film, more than we could ever decently show.

Out from that doomed town came 4000 guiltless, helpless refugees, fleeing from a war that nobody had ever bothered to explain to them. We filmed but we did not interfere. We let them pass. This was not the time for interviews or intrusion. A girl of about eighteen was comforting her father, her arms about his waist, and came to the camera sobbing. 'They have killed every-thing we loved, everyone we loved, there is nothing left here now. But tell them we do not hate them . . . we have no hate left . . . tell them we forgive them.' We did not know it then, but the Serbs had no time for forgiveness.

An old campaigner and great colleague, the BBC's Martin Bell, was waiting on the airstrip at Sarajevo as we taxied to a halt. He was dressed, as usual, in a cricket jumper, a spotless white suit and green socks; they are his lucky charms though he will never tell you why. Though no more eccentric than the rest of us, he is the most superstitious person I have ever known. He is a private man, not one to waste words in either his conversation or his commentaries. He writes like someone picking prize fruit, with great care, knowing, as only a few do, the impact of the well-placed word alongside the well-shot picture, and he has never been short of either. Martin was nicknamed 'Pacer' because he is incapable of standing still for more than a minute. He was the doyen of all journalists who came to Sarajevo, so it was a comfort to see him there waiting so casually, giving the impression that all was well when we all suspected it was not. A few weeks before, he had been awarded the OBE, but had not managed to get back to Buckingham Palace for the Queen to pin it on him. I had bought a miniature medal from Spinks of St James's and I meant to pin it on him, given the right moment and a bottle of whisky. That opportunity presented itself sooner than I expected.

It had been a harrowing day. Two mortar rounds had drop-ped into a narrow street near the river and the market – the Serbs were fond of sending in their shells when they knew people were out searching for fresh water and food. Thirteen people had been killed outright, dozens more were critically wounded; among the casualties were eight small children, play-ing while their mothers were shopping. Their little bodies were left in the street until it was safe to fetch them. No one was fool enough to dare break cover and pick up the dead, whoever they were.

That evening we did what we often needed to do after such experiences: we sat in the dark and drank whisky. Unexpectedly, Martin joined us. He, too, had had a bad day, indeed it had very nearly been his last. Gradually, reluctantly, he told us how close he had come, an hour before, to being killed. He and his cameraman were leaving the airport when two bullets hit their car, one through the open driver's window, passing between them and lodging itself in the doorpost; the second came in between Martin's legs and hit the gearbox.

Taking the last of my whisky, he said: 'You survive one day, you start again tomorrow and you just ignore the law of averages!' It was a remark typical of anyone who works this trade. It was the motto, almost word for word, of Maggie Moth. She was CNN's camerawoman in Sarajevo and, like Martin, thought nothing of staying there for two months at a stretch, while the rest of us flipped anxiously in and out every fortnight or so. She did not believe that the longer the stay the greater the risk; like Martin, she did not believe in odds. That is, until the day a sniper's bullet took away her tongue and lower jaw.

The drive from the airport to Sarajevo's television station was only about two miles but as every reporter or cameraman who has travelled them will agree, they were the longest and most dangerous miles anywhere in the world.

Serb (and sometimes Muslim) snipers positioned themselves at intervals along the route, especially near to roads blocked by burnt-out vehicles. As you slowed down, you gave them an easier target. We named it 'Sniper's Alley'. Some days before I arrived that July, an ITN reporter and cameraman had a bullet come through the back of their car window, pass between them and go out, shattering the front windscreen. They said they could smell the cordite. Next day our second cameraman, Seb

Rich, was hit by a ricochet in the chest; only his flak-jacket saved him. Shortly afterwards, the ABC producer David Kaplan was killed when a sniper's round hit him in the back. No war this half-century has been so deadly, the rate of killing faster than in Vietnam, including casualties among those reporting it. Over fifty reporters and cameramen have died and as many have been injured – more, incredibly, than for all the years spent covering the American war in Vietnam.

Sarajevo quickly won its reputation as a lethal place to work and yet the world's press came to cover it eagerly. The majority of the journalists were British, as is always the case, though no one quite knew why. One Frenchman said it was because the British are naturally warlike and are drawn to wars wherever and for whatever reason they are fought. Perhaps he is right, but all Europeans, in their bones, somewhere and at some time know something of war and the associated horrors of bombing and the inhumanity of those who come to conquer.

Some of us had covered many wars before . . . Yugoslavia was my fourteenth. Going to war, with death as the matter-of-fact reason for being there, had been my occupation for twenty-five years and in that time I had covered more than any other international correspondent. It has been a bloody, dangerous and often very lonely life. A telephone call from ITN's foreign desk and a few hours' flying-time later you are witness to murder in Nigeria and genocide in Biafra, rape in the Congo and a convoy of corpses in the Lebanon . . .

It was part and parcel of the job to be bombed in Vietnam, kidnapped in Beirut, held hostage in Angola. It was my lot to record the cannabalism in Cambodia, to shake hands with the first Turkish paratrooper landing in Cyprus, hold a dying Israeli soldier's hand in the war of Yom Kippur, watch a black bleeding red in Soweto, travel the Ho Chi Minh Trail. I had been threatened by the Palestinians, attacked by the Kyhmer Rouge, besieged by the Indians, ambushed by Cubans. I had been among the last out from Phnom Penh and Saigon, I had seen the drop of a flag and a royal salute turn warring Rhodesia into infant Zimbabwe, sailed 10,000 miles on a British warship to watch men who had been allies kill each other so that bleak and wintry Antarctic islands might again be called the Falklands. And I had spent two months aboard a Royal Navy destroyer in the Persian Gulf when America's war-machine reduced a mad dictator's army to cinders.

I have spent a career watching and writing about men who fight wars, the winners and the losers, the brave and the not so brave, the wise as well as the foolish, the leaders and the led, the few who see war as an entertaining, thrilling spectacle and those who promote them for their own political profit. War is about the many who are slaughtered pointlessly, anonymously, and the many, many more who live through them cowed and fearful and shocked by their survival. Blood, sweat and tears flow in abundance, with the international press corps always chasing, on the heels of every new conflict, every new declaration of hostilities, re-affirming the old saying that 'War makes rattling good history and Peace poor reading'.

Every war is different so there is no single golden rule except to stay alive. A dead reporter has absolutely no worth unless he was selfless enough to bequeath a generous life insurance to dependents. The best advice to the newcomer is never to stop worrying. Anxiety keeps you alive and the man who does not look worried simply does not know what is going on. Yet, despite all my experience of war, I was not prepared for Yugoslavia's.

The *Guardian* correspondent Ed Vulliamy wrote at the time: 'When the veterans of Vietnam, Afghanistan, Lebanon and all the other places came to Yugoslavia, they were rather like uncles at first. But it became clear they were as lost as we were.' There was no front line, no demarcation, the geography of conflict was a hotch-potch, changing by the hour without warning, so that you could never say, 'This is as far as I'll go . . . as far as I'm prepared to risk it.'

They say that only fools and first-timers go into dangerous situations knowingly, that wise men calculate the odds and equate the worth of the story with the risk. I wish it were that simple. Certainly, in Sarajevo, it was not possible to be so logical, so confidently cautious. The only safe place was the cellar and although some newspapermen can still write very plausible accounts of war from such bomb-proof sanctuaries, the television man has to be up front where it is happening every day for as long as it is light and for as long as the television satellite is beckoning. So it was not long into the siege of Sarajevo before reporters and cameramen were wearing bullet-proof vests and helmets and riding in armour-plated cars. ITN's was a redundant police car from Belfast and weighed 3 tons.

Finding somewhere to stay became more of a problem as less of the city became available to us and more and more hotels were destroyed. Those who came early in the year stayed at the Beograd in Princip Street in the Austro-Hungarian centre of the city but that was one of the first casualties. Most of the press corps then shifted to the Bosna in the Serbian-held suburb of Ilidza, built in the grounds of an old hunting lodge where the Archduke Franz Ferdinand stayed in June 1914, the night before his assassination. Then it was the Bosna's turn to be evacuated after a direct hit by Muslim rockets, one of them demolishing the BBC's editing-room. Finally, the Sarajevo Holiday Inn, which had been forced to close in peacetime because it was bankrupt, reopened for the war, and even though one by one its upper floors were very efficiently gutted by Serb shell, rocket and mortar, it remained the headquarters and rest-rooms for the world's press. And despite it all, there was never a shortage of guests.

It was surprising how quickly newcomers adapted to a different kind of normality. After a few days, they reached for their flak-jackets as casually as they would put on a raincoat. When their turn came, few hesitated to go to a job that threatened to cut short a promising career. To many it was their first war and there was much excitement. They were like teenagers attending their first bull-fight, some seeing a warm corpse for the first time, hearing the zing of shrapnel and marvelling at their coolness under fire. They had yet to realize that courage comes easily at first because the unreality of close death provides a mental shield. These bullets are not meant for you, you are a non-combatant, a spectator, on nobody's side. Time and again, that sense of unreality has helped inject massive doses of Dutch courage until the moment when someone is killed close by and the shield is shattered for ever. Is it machismo or masochism that encourages people to risk their lives so compulsively and repeatedly? Perhaps they would like to believe that survival or death is a fluke anyway. The one thing war correspondents have in common is a colossal sense of fatalism, like the GIs in Vietnam who laughingly boasted they were only worried by the bullet with their name on it, though there were the few who worried more about the bullet that had 'To whom it concerns' written on it!

War reporting has been described as the contemporary man's duel. When the newsman comes back from the front, from the challenge, real or unreal, of enemy fire, he feels the same pounding in his blood as any soldier. So it was in Sarajevo. The first decision of the day was whether to get up and go out into those streets at war, in the full and certain knowledge that it could be the last decision you ever made. It was all made easier by the camera crew, the cameraman and his sound-recordist, the two men you trusted to do the necessary with the minimum of fuss. Morning tea was drunk, camera gear assembled, notebook and pens pocketed, flak-jackets and helmets donned, fingers crossed. Then into the car to begin another day at war and that first dash along the most fearful road in the world.

Diary entry: Monday, 6 July

My fifth day in Sarajevo. The city is waiting for a lull. The Serbs are determined there should be none. This morning they sent in five mortar shells, placed to do the most damage, timed to kill the most effectively, just as the early shoppers were in the market-place. Ten had been killed but the toll could be much higher because the hospitals are crowded and the wounded will have to wait their turn. The hospitals have been hit so many times, only the ground floors and basements are safe to use. 440 beds have been reduced to 150 and of the original 550 doctors and nurses, there is now only room for 120. Medicines are being rationed to the young and only those who have any chance to recover. In the past week, two convoys, one French and one United Nations, have got through but a few lorries make little difference and there is now the very real prospect that Sarajevo will be starved to surrender. People are buying grass and dock leaves and rotting cabbages in the market, what they once gave to their cows. But if that is what you eat to survive, that is what you buy. We filmed in the cemetery today, or rather what passes as one because the main one is full now and they are beginning to bury their dead in football pitches. Difficult to believe, but in the past three months of siege nearly 2000 people have been killed here and 9000 wounded. And how absurd. Only today the Bosnian government has at last admitted it is at a state of war!

That evening we were returning from Sarajevo's television station after a News at Ten satellite feed when a lone and very accurate sniper refused to let us into our bombed-out hotel at the far end of Sniper's Alley close to the city centre. Every time we poked our heads around the wall he fired, the bullets splitting bricks only a few yards away. It seemed a pointless and rather murderous game of cat and mouse. We waited there for an hour, he obviously enjoying his deadly sport, we becoming ever anxious at the prospect of being left out on our own unprotected and at the mercy of all sides once the night's routine fighting began. Finally, somebody radioed for a UN armoured car, and once its commander had trained his heavy machine-gun on the sniper's hide-out, we managed the 100-yard sprint without another shot being fired.

But my cameraman Seb Rich, not satisfied with surviving another day, decided to try his luck into the night and went up on to the hotel roof to film the same sniper's position from a few hundred yards away. A half-hour later, as we were finishing what passed as dinner, he came down, his face covered in blood. The sniper had sighted him and fired back, shattering a glass window. Dowsing Seb with vodka, the only disinfectant we had with us, and with others holding him steady, I pulled a sliver of glass nearly 3 inches long from his chin; the tip had pierced his eardrum and his face looked as if it was ready to burst.

We reported the incident to our news managers in London and they decided, as we knew they would, that the story was not worth another casualty. Seb was ordered out on the next morning's returning relief flight for treatment in Zagreb and I was told to evacuate by road to Belgrade, the Serbian capital, and await further instructions.

Thus my first visit to Sarajevo ended abruptly with no guarantee that I would return very soon. Yet within days I would be back and a new adventure would begin, with fate arranging a rendezvous with a little girl who would change my life.

CHAPTER TWO

'**D**amn the idiots!'
It was a one-line entry in my diary dated Thursday, 9 July. I had just received a fax from ITN London ordering me back to Sarajevo with a new camera crew although I had only just arrived in Belgrade, exhausted after a twelve-hour drive across the mountains and through dozens of Serbian military road-blocks. At every one I had patiently gone through the same security charade, producing my passport, Serbian press card, ITN identity and government travel papers, opening an empty car boot a dozen times in as many miles to assure successive militiamen that I was not a gun-runner. It reminded me of Beirut many years before, where roads were shared out among the Palestinians, the Christians and the Syrians, like ancient toll-roads and just as lucrative. They were often manned by arrogant teenage Rambos festooned with firepower, carrying a mixture of Soviet and American weapons, wearing 'Kiss me Baby' T-shirts and designer jeans, their hair well-oiled, and smelling of after-shave or marijuana or both. They enjoyed their roles as non-combatant road wardens, collecting dues in dollars or camera equipment, prodding sensitive parts with their highly polished automatics and massaging their grenades. Wise men did what they were told.

Off again to Sarajevo, but first a day's shopping in Belgrade, to fill our vans with fruit and fresh water, candles, dehydrated and vacuum-packed meals and those extra cans of diesel because there was no fuel beyond the Serbian lines. My camera crew, Jon Martin and Russ Padwick, were driving down from Budapest. Because of the UN trade embargo on Serbia, all international flights to Belgrade were banned. Jon and Russ would have a day's drive, a few hours' sleep, and then we would begin another day's drive south together. Despite all my years' experience of it, I wondered once more at how casually our editors toss us around the globe. Perhaps they glance at the map of the world and reduce vast, difficult and frequently dangerous distances to an inch of coloured paper!

I once worked for a news editor whose job it was to send men such distances. His office was full of nostalgic junk, mementos of yesterday's scoops and beats and all those things that had made his beginner's days in television news so exciting and pioneering. There was an Israeli infantryman's helmet from the Yom Kippur war, complete with the hole through which a Syrian bullet had passed; a transistor radio made as a convincing replica of a hand-grenade and sold in the streets of civil war Beirut; and a tricolour taken by the British army on the day they finally flushed the IRA out of Crossmaglen, Northern Ireland. He had a large *Daily Telegraph* wall map into which he stabbed tiny coloured pins wherever his veterans made yet another corner of a foreign field forever England. It was so old that it still showed places like Rhodesia and Leopoldville and Lorenco Marques, and he would measure distances with his hand, digging his thumb into London and sliding his outstretched palm across Europe, skimming the Alps, spanning the Mediterranean, North Africa and down over Ethiopia and the Horn, thumb to little finger like a crawling crab, on into the Indian Ocean. Then, with a deft twist of the wrist, he hand-crawled due south. By the map's legend, his span equalled 1000 miles, so London to Madagascar was just over 5500 hand-miles. He considered his method of measurement infallible.

Friday, 10 July and we hear bad news as we leave Belgrade. The BBC World Service is reporting that UN relief flights into Sarajevo have been cancelled because of renewed fighting around the airport which we must cross to get into the city. This adds to our anxiety because the fighting may spread, blocking our way, and it is essential for us to be back over the mountains in good time to report to the UN sentry post on the Serbian side of the airport while it is still light. Crossing no man's land after dark would be suicidal. Even if the Serb patrols let us pass, we would have to run the gauntlet first of the maverick Serb snipers, then the Muslim gunners, then the notoriously volatile Croat road-blocks, and finally make peace with the Bosnian patrols inside the city limits. Three separate armies, each prepared to destroy their land rather than let a morsel of it go to the other and fighting under the tricolour of nationalism, religion and greed.

Yugoslavia had for decades been by far the most approachable of all the European Communist countries. Visitors, mostly Western tourists, admired what they saw there and what its President-for-Life Josip Broz – 'Tito' – appeared to have achieved. He had bonded so many different peoples into a workable, national mix, transcending, or so it seemed then, the ethnic rivalries that bedevilled so many other countries. Who visiting Yugoslavia at that time, on business, sailing, skiing, touring, could possibly have guessed it would soon be torn apart so brutally, so tragically, so swiftly?

Yugoslavia, 'land of the South Slavs', was a country of six republics, five peoples, four languages, three religions and two alphabets, but with a benevolent dictator and a Communist Party which kept this mongrel nation with its two most volatile elements, the Serbs and the Croats, obedient and passive. Serbs and Croats had long been bitter rivals, hostile and suspicious of each other's determination to dominate, the Serbs resentful at the Croats' propensity to make trouble. The Serbs in the east of the country had for centuries been kept apart from the Croats, mainly in the west, by a constantly shifting military frontier. Like the fault-line of an earthquake region, this divided Eastern from Western Europe, separating not only two cultures but two

Empires, those of the Hapsburgs and the Ottoman Turks.

The two tribes share the same language but have little else in common. The Serbs are Orthodox Christians whose religion was crucial in keeping their national identity alive during almost four centuries of Ottoman occupation. The Croats were ruled by the Austrians and Hungarians, and their Catholicism and self-consciously Western attitudes were just as important in shaping their nationalism. Although kept apart by their separate rulers, both Hapsburg and Ottoman did their worst to stoke mutual hatreds, especially in those areas where Serb and Croat overlapped.

The ferocity of the Balkan peoples has at times been so primitive that anthropologists have likened them to the Amazon's Yanomamo, one of the world's most savage and primitive tribes. Up until the turn of the present century, when the rest of Europe was concerned as much with social etiquette as with social reform, there were still reports from the Balkans of decapitated enemy heads presented as trophies on silver plates at victory dinners. Nor was it unknown for the winners to eat the loser's heart and liver. As late as 1903, the King and Queen of Serbia were murdered by their trusted guards who then hacked them to bits and threw the pieces to the crowd in the streets below the palace bedchamber. Apologists blame such savagery on the Ottoman Turks, who ruled much of the Balkans until 1912 and used massacre as an instrument of government. But the history books show it as a land of murder and revenge before the Turks arrived and long after they departed.

The disintegration of Tito's Yugoslavia was not just the legacy of the Ottomans. The hatreds and vendettas had their origin in both ancient tribalism and modern politics. Before the outbreak of the present civil war, the Second World War had seemed the apogee of this mutual hatred. When the Nazis overran the country in 1941, they set up a Croatian Fascist puppet state which the majority of Croats at first supported. Croats fought alongside the Germans, though many, like Tito himself, fought as partisans with the Allies. Encouraged by the Nazis'

example, the Fascist Croats began their own pogrom of exterminating Serbs, Jews and gypsies, and it is estimated that more
than a half a million were killed in the four years to the end of
the war. Today there is still a memorial at Donja Gradina to the
360,000 Serbs who were clubbed to death, decapitated, hanged
or stabbed by zealots of the Fascist 'Ustasha' army. Railway
waggons that brought them from the Jasenovac concentration
camp are still there, macabre monuments to appalling cruelty.
The Jasenovac camp, close to the Sava river, covered an area of
over 200 square kilometres, which made it far, far bigger than
the Nazi camps at Belsen and Auschwitz. The Nazi war criminal
Adolf Eichmann later publicly congratulated the Croats for
'radically resolving the Jewish . . . and other problems'.

Once the blood was in the water, the accumulated hatred of
centuries developed its own momentum and today there is not a
town or village in the region that does not have its own chilling
memories. Not that the Croats did all the killing. The Serbs also
used the war to have their revenge and rid themselves of those
they considered ethnically unacceptable. Today young extremists still sing a song made infamous a half-century ago: 'The
Bloody River Drina, Pride of the Serbs', reminding those who
wish to be reminded of the Serb slaughter of 50,000 Muslims at
Foca in 1943.

Tito, of mixed Croat–Slovenian stock, came to power at the
end of the war. His strategy was to bury ethnic hatreds under
the cloak of Yugoslav nationalism, creating a federation of six
republics – Croatia, Serbia, Bosnia, Slovenia, Macedonia and
Montenegro. By using the age-old tactic of divide and rule, he
cunningly promoted the ethnic minorities in some Republics
and the majorities in others to positions of power, creating a
weighted balance of interests, so that despite the tensions, he
held his country together for thirty-five years. Whenever necessary, his diktats were reinforced by the harshness of Communist
rule and the ruthlessness of his secret police. And after Tito's
break with Moscow in 1948, and with Stalin hovering on the doorstep, sticking together was generally thought a wise thing to do.

With Tito's death in 1980, the cracks began to show. Factions formed within the Communist Parties of the various republics and they began looking for popular support among their constituents, not to destroy Yugoslavia but to establish more autonomy for themselves. But having once appealed to ethnic pride and prejudice, there was no going back. With the end of the Cold War and the collapse of East European Communism from 1989 onwards, nationalism ran like lava into every crack and cranny of Tito's Yugoslavia, and the edifice, like the Berlin Wall, began to crumble.

Until then, the potential dissolution of Yugoslavia had never been a subject for much other than academic seminars. It was generally agreed that the country was in need of a shake-up not a break-up, and that could be comfortably achieved by cutting the army budget and giving the balance to the Republics to spend on new factories, tourist resorts and basketball teams. That, along with more devolution, would soon end the grumblings. It might well have done had the Serb Slobodan Milosevic not had ambitions of his own. It is said that he was the first Yugoslav politician to realize that Tito was dead, and his ambition was not only to inherit Tito's power but to use the federal army and the Communist Party to transform the carefully balanced Yugoslavia into a Serb-dominated state.

The alarm bells rang. The republics wanted greater autonomy and the release of their nationalism to follow the direction in which the rest of the old Eastern bloc was running. But that was not what the Serbs in Belgrade had in mind.

It was now only a matter of time, and on 25 June 1991, the political time-bomb exploded. Slovenia, one of the smaller republics but also the richest, and sitting protectively under the wing of Austria, declared its independence as a sovereign state. Some hours later, Croatia did the same. The Serbs in Belgrade reacted the only way they knew how; they sent in the tanks. By dawn on the 27th, the border-crossing between Slovenia and Austria at Sentilj was ablaze. The federal air force had bombed what it thought was a Slovenian barricade of lorries but it was a civilian freight convoy and ten Turkish drivers were burned alive by mistake.

The European Community, facing its first European war since its inception, was confused. Instead of accepting the inevitable break-up of Yugoslavia and concentrating its diplomacy on protecting the rights of vulnerable minorities, it warned the two republics against secession. The Serbs interpreted this as non-recognition of the two break-aways and it provided Milosevic with exactly the excuse he wanted to recover what he had so unexpectedly lost. Accepting Slovenia's *de facto* independence, he turned his fury on Croatia.

Over half a million Serbs lived in Croatia, concentrated mainly in the Dalmatian hinterland of Krijina. On the pretext that the Croats were about to repeat their wartime atrocities against them, the federal army, now Serb-dominated, invaded with the biggest movement of tanks, guns and men seen in Europe since the Second World War. That July and August, they sliced through northern Dalmatia, destroying towns and villages as they carved out new enclaves. Some of their offensives were made simply out of spite and the desire to destroy anything non-Serb. The medieval fortress port of Dubrovnik was one such example. This architectural gem of the Adriatic was put under siege and suffered relentless bombardment. Vukovar, on the Danube, was surrounded and finally erased. From the centre the army pushed north from Pakrac towards the Hungarian border to create another Serb enclave.

Croatia was diminished daily. By Christmas, it had lost nearly a third of its territory with hundreds of towns and villages destroyed. Its lucrative tourist trade had come to a complete halt, with millions in hard currency lost every day. And yet, instead of deterring Croatian independence, the aggression established it. The Croats printed their own currency, their own passports, set up their own airline and sent heads of missions to the world's capitals. They created an army which grew rapidly in size and strength despite the UN embargo; traffic in arms across the Austrian border was as busy as it was blatant.

Soon the war came to a standstill and in the New Year, Slobodan Milosevic accepted the stalemate and the international mediation that followed. In January 1992, both sides signed the peace plan for Croatia, brokered by the American Cyrus Vance, and 14,000 UN troops were promptly dispatched with a mandate to oversee the withdrawal of the federal army and ensure the safe return of hundreds of thousands of displaced refugees. The army left but today, nearly two years on, we are still awaiting the completion of the other task.

Slovenian and Croatian independence created an imbalance within what was left of Yugoslavia. The ever-resourceful President Milosevic decided on a way to resolve it. The third largest republic, Bosnia, would join a rump Yugoslavia, ruled by him. Another time-bomb had been fused. The Bosnian government denounced it, but with its squabbling mixture of Serb, Croatian and Muslim ministers, it could not respond to the catastrophe all saw approaching. The $1\frac{1}{2}$ million Bosnian Serbs, a third of the population, sensing a move towards a declaration of Bosnian independence and determined to thwart it, declared a number of autonomous provinces whose allegiance was to Belgrade not Sarajevo. They declared they were now part of Greater Serbia, the centuries-old dream finally to be realized. The non-Serb Bosnians (2 million Muslims and 700,000 Croats) were anxious not to provoke the Serbs, having seen what they had done in Croatia. The Bosnian President Alija Izetbegovic called a referendum in February, to decide the independence issue, and two-thirds of the vote endorsed it. The Serbs, who were already being secretly armed by Milosevic, boycotted it, and a month later barricaded the main routes in and out of Sarajevo. Then, in that first week of April last year, their patience at an end, thousands of people from this city's mixed population came on to the streets to dismantle the barricades, some shouting for peace, some for independence, and many carrying pictures of Tito. From the roof of the Holiday Inn, a Serb sniper shot dead a girl student. She was the first casualty of the Bosnian war.

Bosnia had traditionally been known as the powder-keg of the Balkans because of its explosive ethnic mix. The Serbs especially had always regarded it as rightfully theirs and were outraged when, after centuries of Turkish rule, it was annexed by the Austro-Hungarians in 1908. The Croats were gratified, expecting Vienna to hand it to them. To avenge the wrong, a young Serb nationalist, Gavrilo Princip, shot dead the heir to the Hapsburg Empire, the Archduke Franz Ferdinand, when he visited Sarajevo on Serbian National Day in 1914. The assassination triggered the First World War.

President Milosevic was determined to subvert Bosnia's bid for independence. He had to bring all of Bosnia to heel if he was to keep together what was left of his Yugoslavia, or at the very least detach as much of it as he could for himself. So he dispatched his gauleiters to create alarm throughout the towns and countryside of Bosnia, where Serb and non-Serb slept side by side and sometimes together. Messengers from Belgrade whispered their black propaganda that the Muslims were about to create a Bosnian Fundamentalist Islamic Republic where all children would have their heads shaved, the boys circumcised and all women wear purdah. They distorted phrases used in an academic essay, 'Islamic Declaration', written years before by President Izetbegovic, as evidence that Sarajevo was to become another Teheran, with ferocious mullahs issuing fatwas.

To anyone who knew the Bosnian Muslims, such claims were absurd. These people were the most moderate, least extremist, most Westernized of any of the Islamic faith, and Sarajevo itself had been known for generations as the most civilized and tolerant place in the Balkans, one of the great homes of European cosmopolitan culture. Forty years of Communism had produced the most secular and integrated Muslims in the world. Intermarriage between Muslims and people of other faiths was commonplace. Even Jewish Muslim marriages were not unheard of and had it not been for the Nazi occupation there would probably have been more. Sarajevo, like Bosnia, had no reason to go to war with itself on any ethnic pretext, because, despite history's geographical and religious divisions, no ethnic difference existed among the Orthodox Christian Serbs, the Catholic Croats and the Bosnian Muslims.

Yet the crude ruse to generate hatred against the Muslims worked, and fear and revenge provided a murderous momentum as the Croats too saw their opportunity to kill and seize land after rummaging for an historical reason to do so. From a state in which Bosnian Serbs and Croats and Muslims had lived for most of this century at peace, side by side, house by house, village by village, in towns and in cities, they began to murder each other, rape their neighbours' wives and daughters, castrate their neighbours' sons. An ancient hatred had been tragically refired by the political mind-benders in Belgrade.

So Bosnia began its journey along the road to dusty death. The Muslims, who needed Yugoslavia more than any other of the South Slavs, might better have stayed even in a rump Yugoslavia, if their special identity could have been protected. Now they were fighting for their very survival against two merciless attackers.

The UN pleaded to both sides not to change the map by force, but the Balkan people had rarely seen it changed any other way. Serb and Croat alike knew they would get most of what they wanted by the time-honoured method. And, in due course, they did.

Now, on the road south from Belgrade, en route to Sarajevo, we were witnessing just how efficiently the Serbs were going about achieving their objective. We were seeing for ourselves what a few daring reporters had already reported before us. They had revealed to a still disinterested world, two unfamiliar words that described something most familiar and sinister, a phrase that now entered the vocabulary of war as 'ethnic cleansing'.

When I had driven north from Sarajevo two days before, I had noticed that many of the small towns and villages on the

way were deserted, something I had assumed to be simple pre-
cautions by wary residents retreating to the safer hinterland.
Now, coming back, seeing the same villages and small towns in
daylight, the realization of what had happened to them stunned
me. In the farmyards there were a few pigs and chickens, goats
and cows, there was a tractor with its trailerload of hay parked
awkwardly at a crossroads, and in the back gardens we could
see clothes hanging from the washing-lines. There was little
damage to the houses, just the occasional shell-hole in a
scorched roof or the splatter of machine-gun fire against the
stucco. But there were no people.

'Muslims,' said Jacko, our driver and interpreter, 'gone.'

'Gone where?' we asked.

'Gone who knows where,' said Jacko, but Jacko knew.
Jacko was a Serb and the Serbs knew what was happening to
the Muslims, just as during the Second World War so many
Germans must have known what was happening to the Jews.

The Serbs were forcibly evacuating the Bosnian Muslims
from their homes and land to 'cleanse' the area for their own
people. They worked it this way. As they took control of a
Muslim area, they went from house to house demanding an
oath of loyalty from every family member including the
children. Most would not give this, as for Muslims it would be
denouncing their faith, and so they were sent in lorries to detention centres, the men to one, the women and children to
another. Many were destined never to see each other again.
At the centres, they were forced to sign away their property,
promising never to return to their homes again. The lucky ones
were then taken by truck to the Croatian border and dumped
there as refugees at the mercy of international charity. In this
way, the Serbs quickly rid themselves of the Muslims so that the
land and farms, houses and shops and businesses could be given
free to Serbs.

Not all who went to the camps left them alive, however. We
do not know how many were killed and guessing serves no
purpose, but we do know from eye-witnesses and independent

sources that many, many Muslims were killed simply because it was more practicable and less costly than to transport them elsewhere. Where logistics were difficult, slaughter was the answer. The massacre of more than 200 Muslim prisoners, men and young boys, by Serb militia at the edge of a ravine near Travnik is recorded as one such cruel expediency. Semir was twenty-four. He was arrested in the town of Carakovo and taken to the Trnopolje detention camp and beaten until he could not see for his own blood. Some days later he was taken by lorry with another 200 or more men and boys and told they were being exchanged for Serb prisoners of war. The lorries stopped at what Semir knew to be the River Ugar.

> I was in the middle of the lorry and as men were taken off
> I heard shots, then they came back for more. We realized
> it was over for us, there was no life. They started taking
> people by threes and we heard machine-gun bursts as well
> as pistol shots. The guard nudged me with his rifle and told
> me to take two with me but when I rose I looked and my
> little brother Sakib and my nephew were lying on the floor
> crying. I decided to run, whatever happened. I pushed the
> soldier, three steps was all I needed to jump into the gorge.
> I landed on a tree, I thought my left arm was broken.
> There were dead bodies all around me, hanging from the
> branches. As I jumped again, the soldiers fired and I fell
> and stayed still on my back. They heaved more bodies down,
> the skull of one of them burst on a rock near me and his
> brain splattered my face. I did not dare move and watched
> them sling the bodies into the canyon. It took more than
> an hour.

It had started to rain as we began our final climb over the mountains beyond the Serb headquarters town of Pale. Rain was both a curse and a blessing, the former because it would make the drive doubly dangerous, with the track already a quagmire churned up by the tanks; the latter because we hoped the snipers we feared more than anything would prefer to spend their evening dry indoors.

We were right on the first count: we slid and spun our way up past the tank emplacements and the field guns, their barrels pointing to the sky in a trajectory towards Sarajevo. But despite the rain-storm, we managed to reach the mountain's highest point with an hour of daylight to spare, which meant we should make the UN post with enough time for the crossing. Through the rain, we could just make out Sarajevo below us, like a large-scale relief map, with the runway to the left, the brown sprawl of the Muslim enclave of Dobrinia immediately below us, and to the right, the dark line we knew as Sniper's Alley, the main airport road leading to the besieged city's centre.

The evening's shelling had already begun. We heard the howitzers' booms from somewhere along the ridge to our right, only a mile or so away, and seconds later saw the flashes of orange in the city below. There was the familiar low rumble and rattle as tanks manoeuvred into new night-time positions, readying themselves for another night's bombardment. How strange and how perverse that we were so anxious to travel so quickly to be at their receiving end! We tied to the van's radio aerial a white pillow-case we had 'borrowed' from the hotel and spread an oversize Union Jack across the roof so that hopefully no one would be in any doubt who we were.

As any motorist knows, returning along a road he has recently travelled does not guarantee faultless navigation. Things look different the other way round and that evening, any building I might have recognized was anyway hidden in the greyness of the storm. Yet I knew we dared not get it wrong. We had to find the UN post, to make contact with the sentries there and have them radio to the control tower for clearance to cross the runway. There was no other way. In the half-light we would not be able to turn back to the Serbs, but if we failed to go forward we would be marooned in no man's land, everyone's target and most especially of the snipers with their high-velocity rifles, telescopic sights and murderous intent.

For half an hour I drove through the rain trying to find my way, lost in the suburbs of a city at war, not knowing who was watching us, waiting. This was the front line, so some streets had to be mined but there was no knowing which, as it is not the habit of any side to advertise where they have buried their deadly high explosives. I stopped, reversed, swung the steering wheel, spun the wheels with the engine racing, filled with the sudden certainty that we were about to be blown up. I accelerated into a dead end, tried a new direction at the next turn and found the road blocked by a burnt-out lorry. And all this time Jon, Russ and Jacko said nothing but sank deeper into their seats, pulled the collars of their flak-jackets over their ears, and prayed.

Then, through the splashing movement of the windscreen wipers, I saw what we were after, the silhouette of an armoured personnel carrier, the UN post. A soldier ran up to us, wearing the comforting blue beret and 'CANADA' on his shoulder-flash.

'There's been some firing,' he shouted above the wind. 'We've had some rounds in ourselves – pretty close. You'd best wait till morning.'

'That's not possible, we'll never find our way back to the mountain road now. Please radio for permission to cross.' He did and the answer came back: 'Affirmative but on their own heads be it', which was not what we wanted to hear. The armoured car moved back and he waved us through.

'Keep going till you can go no more, then turn left and make for the hangars . . . but for Christ's sake go fast and keep it going.'

He did not know it but he almost sent us to our deaths. Many times since I have thought of that moment, trying to remember his exact words, wondering whether I misheard them or whether, as I would like to believe, he got it wrong in the confusion of the storm, having just survived an attack himself. Because we went too far. Driving at top speed, even though we could see little in the rain, we overshot the main runway's left turn and carried on until we were at the perimeter, at the very edge of the field. And there ahead of us, less than 50 yards away, were the derelict and partly demolished houses that provided the hideaways, lookout posts and sniper positions for the men who killed so expertly, so indiscriminately, so often.

Suddenly the rain stopped and so did we. But there was no panic now, no reason to charge left or right, no escape route. Spinning the back wheels, revving the engine, frantic three-point turns could serve no purpose now. We were in full view of anyone who wanted to kill us, a big white Dormobile van with what suddenly seemed such a silly mud-splashed pillow-case and such a gaudy, tawdry, sodden flag. We had meant them to protect us. Now they were a provocation and an invitation to fire.

I reversed slowly, taking my time, waiting for the wind-screen and side windows to shatter, waiting for the first of the many bullets. I thought of Martin Bell and the night we had shared our last whisky and I thought of Maggie Moth and the scaffolding of wire and pins that was holding her face together. I thought, in those brief moments, of all those I had seen critically wounded, men who had watched their own blood drain from them, knowing they were already dead. I remembered a friend, a combat cameraman from Vietnam, who had said to me, 'I am not afraid of being killed but I don't want to be wounded and lie out there with a gut full of shrapnel waiting to die . . . I really don't care for it at all.'

All this passed across the mind's eye as I waited for the executioner's axe to fall. But it did not, and I shall never know why. We drove away from those houses, still expecting bullets to follow us right up to the moment we arrived safely outside the UN headquarters building.

'That's the dumbest thing I have ever seen *anyone* do,' said a Canadian voice beneath a blue beret.

'God knows why they didn't hit you,' someone else said.

'The luck of the British,' said another.

'Welcome to Sarajevo,' said the Frenchman, smiling.

For seemingly no particular reason that night saw one of the heaviest bombardments of the city so far and we considered it a bad omen. Rockets and mortars were landing right by the hotel, cameramen spent their night on the roof filming apartment blocks taking direct hits only a few hundred yards away, homes with people still in them were demolished, sides of buildings falling away like wet cement from a wall. Our own bedrooms had been made into makeshift shelters, mattresses and wardrobes pushed up against the windows to reduce the blast and save us from a thousand glass splinters that could tear a man to shreds. Many of the press slept fully dressed in the corridors, ready to evacuate at a second's notice, such was their fear of being trapped on the upper floors by fire.

Through the hole in the wall that used to be my window, I could see east towards the old quarter of the city and the fighting there was ferocious, the sky bright with explosions and parachute flares and the criss-crossing arcing of tracer rounds, such awesome pyrotechnics, that we might easily have forgotten we were witnessing other men and women's deaths at safe remove. Using the tiny beam of a pencil torch, any other light would have attracted a sniper's bullet, I tuned into the BBC World Service just as 'Lillibalero' faded and the Greenwich time signal heralded the start of another day.

> This is London. In Bosnia, Serb forces have launched their biggest offensive in months against the capital Sarajevo, now in its fourth month of siege. Our correspondent reports heavy shelling of the area around the military hospital and that the main civilian hospital has taken a direct hit. Casualties are unknown. Meanwhile . . .

That was my story the next morning and we started on it early. Both hospitals had indeed been hit but as all but the ground and first floors had long been evacuated, there were no casualties, at least not inside the hospitals. There were many from outside. It had indeed been a blitz and the casualty wards and trauma centres were full. We could do nothing but record it and report it.

I began with Belma Goralia. She was twenty-four and had been working in the hospital as a fourth-year medical student.

Asleep in bed that night, a mortar fragment had come through the window and shattered her spine and she would never walk again. In the children's ward, a little baby, six-month-old Kemal, sat curious, kicking vigorously with one leg, and holding the stump of the other, severed from the knee by shrapnel as he lay in the arms of his mother, who was killed by the same explosion. Siad was nine, his thin body entwined in tubes of blood and plasma, a little boy dying, his liver ruptured by grenade fragments. Dudic, four, had every limb in his tiny body broken, his face unrecognizable with burns. And Zenaisa, fifteen, had the prettiest face and the darkest eyes and a body that should not have belonged to her, cut open by splinters of white-hot metal, splinters that had pierced her lungs and stomach and even her heart. We stopped at each in turn and we did as gently as we could what it was our duty to do; record what we saw and show it for the world to pass judgement.

Maggie O'Kane, the *Guardian*'s extraordinarily brave and feisty reporter, wrote of her visit:

> 'There was a fourteen-year-old girl on a bed in the corridor. She was one of twenty people injured in a mortar attack the night before. The doctors were brusque and busy and under terrible pressure and one came along and pulled her shirt back . . . and she had lost a breast. It's one of the few times I've really cried. You see big soldiers, big messy men with wounds and you don't feel the same thing. But I saw this young woman with beautiful skin and beautiful hair and a new young breast blown away . . .'

It was not easy. It gets harder to cope. Experience is no comforter. Age softens you. The more you see, the more it hurts and the greater the difficulty to be objective, to remember that rule of ethics that says reporters must keep to the middle road and report what they see, not what they feel, to report the story, not assume a role in it. But how hard it was that morning to stay on the touchline, as the spectator, trying to keep suffering at arm's length, when it was the children who were suffering the most. What I saw that day all around me was numbing and, like so many reporters then, I began to relish the idea of a concerted allied air attack on the Serbs in the mountains, as clinical and as total as the one that blitzed Saddam's desert army.

'The children must be saved,' the surgeon said to me as we left the wards. 'Whatever else we do, we must save our children, only they are the innocent. The rest of us are the guilty ones.'

Old women were praying by the roadside. It was Sunday but the cathedral was too far to walk to and too close to the sniper line for any but the most devout to risk Mass that morning. A tape-recorded muezzin's call from a minaret in the old quarter close to the river enabled Muslims to kneel in their homes and pay homage to their God in some safety. There was much to pray for and much to be saved from, but Christian and Muslim alike, as they closed their eyes, must have wondered if any of their prayers were being heard.

We had decided that day to film a story of children at an orphanage, high up in one of the suburbs overlooking the city. Our Bosnian guide called them orphans, though no one knew for sure whether their parents were dead or not; it was just assumed they were. In the chaos of a city under siege and bombardment they had been separated from their families, and doubtless there were mothers or fathers still alive who were convinced that their children were dead. What was certain was that until the war ended and families had the chance to find each other again, these children would be classed as orphans and would live as such.

We also saw the abandoned mentally handicapped. Their hostel had been burnt out by incendiary bombs so they lived their days as well as their nights in a cellar. It was sad but it is always the way that in the priorities of survival these people come last, and if it was not for a handful of volunteers, who knows what would have become of them?

The orphanage Ljubica Ivezic is named after a teenage heroine who fought as a partisan with the British against the

Germans in the Second World War. It looked what it was, short of funds, short of everything needed to provide a little joy to the 200 children there. Its director, Vera Zoric, cried on camera as I interviewed her about the children's safety and their future.

'You must tell the United Nations to get them out, otherwise they will die here . . . die from hunger, from cold or killed by the Serbs. Every day they are shelling us, every day they come closer. Already I have buried babies. Tell your people that my children should not die . . . they are not to blame for this.' Because of the fear of mortars, Mrs Zoric kept fifty babies in the basement, all of whom had been abandoned: none was over six months old. The favourites were four boys all aged three months, who had no names but were called by the colour of their jump-suits. There was no fresh water for them, no daylight, and their ration of powdered milk depended on the UN flights arriving daily. None had landed for three days now, and those who cared for them were in despair.

The older children were upstairs in bare dormitories but they assembled cheerily, as children always do, when they saw Jon's camera. There was Miadrag, nine years old and very shy, who did not know whether his parents were alive or dead; no one did. Amelia – the name meant 'clever' – was left by her mother when the fighting began and she had not come back. Romela's mother, father and sister were killed together in the same shelling. Surrounded by them, I was fired by a mixture of anger and my own despair. The children must be saved, the surgeon had asked the world to help and Mrs Zoric had just added her own tearful appeal. I began my commentary to camera:

It is extraordinary, is it not, that there are in this one hostel, upwards of 200 children who could be saved from all this and flown abroad, at least until this war is over. And yet, someone, somewhere along the line says no. At least not yet.'

When I had finished, a little girl came up quietly and stood by me. She watched Jon pack away his camera gear, our visit was over, our story of the orphans of Ljubica Ivezic completed, and within a few hours it would be satellited to London for that evening's News at Ten. She was a pretty girl, with a high fore-head, a tiny upturned nose and deep brown eyes, and I wondered why we had not filmed her with the rest, she was so obviously photogenic. So, irksome though it was for Jon, he unpacked and reset his camera as I knelt beside her. She was very thin and there was a sore at the corner of her mouth. Her dark brown hair was pulled tightly back and tied in a pony-tail. There was a red burn mark on her neck.

'What is your name?' I asked. But before my question was translated she had answered, and with the biggest smile of the day. 'Natasha,' she said. 'Natasha Mihaljcic.'

Through Jacko, our interpreter, she spoke very shyly at first about her life in the orphanage, of the boy bullies who had held a lighted cigarette to her neck, of being more and more fright-ened by the noise of the war as it came closer, and how she and the others in their dormitory beds watched its colours in the night sky through the window in the roof. Like the others, she had compiled her own catalogue of the horrors that had become so much part and parcel of Sarajevo's daily life and she recounted them in the same matter-of-fact way.

We packed up our gear again and prepared to leave. As we said our goodbyes to Mrs Zoric and her staff, Natasha spoke to Jacko. He laughed. Jacko often laughed.

'She wants to know where you are from and I told her England. She says one day she will go to England.' But as I reminded him, all the other orphans had said the same thing.

CHAPTER THREE

I had made a decision. Or rather, it had been made for me. For that past week in my reports to ITN I had complained at the lack of action in rescuing the children under siege, of Western governments turning their backs, paralysed by their confusion at what was happening; of the mainstream international aid organizations like Save the Children and Oxfam so absorbed by African famines that they seemed to care nothing for the suffering on their doorstep; and of the wimpering pundits in their cosy Oxbridge college rooms, declaring as a matter of irrefutable fact that children should not be removed from the land of their birth, whatever their plight, despite the pleading of Sarojevans for their children to be rescued.

Now I had decided to do something myself, something that for all the years past had never been so far away. I would practise what I had been preaching, put my foot where my mouth was, attempt one practical contribution. I would take a child out of Sarajevo and I was already two-thirds of the way into the action.

I had spent much of the past few nights awake, thinking of how it could be done and why. And who? Who would I choose? Who would they choose for me? I thought of little Kemal pondering his lost leg and the dozens of other sick and wounded in the wards around him who could not leave without proper medical company. And I thought of the orphans and Mrs Zoric weeping: 'Tell your people my children should not die . . . they are not to blame for this.'

Maybe it began a long time ago in any one of the dozen places where I had stood at a cameraman's shoulder watching and wanting to do more than just record and report, wanting to assume a role, to participate. Maybe it began at Umburu in Biafra, Christmas 1969, at the height of the starvation. It was television's first famine and Umburu was one of the worst-affected camps, 8 miles from the fighting, with over 4000 children and every one a refugee orphan. They came walking towards us singing, thinking we had brought food, and when they saw we had none they stopped. Then there was a most terrible silence. The priests said that if the war did not end quickly they would all die. It did not, and in what is once again Nigeria, that hideaway camp in the bush is the mass grave of all those innocent little casualties of still-born Biafra.

Or maybe it began in Bihal North in the summer of 1971. The persecution and slaughter of the Bengalis by the Pakistanis was just about complete, done so casually and so callously, and yet so easily forgotten by a forgiving world. The Bengalis who escaped the Pakistani pogrom were dying on countless jungle paths as East Bengal haemorrhaged into India, wretched, despairing columns trudging through the monsoon rain, thick yellow mud sucking their feet, their eyes unblinking in the rain, so weary, that no one, not even the children, bothered to cry. I saw a little boy of about three with his mother who was no more than sixteen or so; they sat down exhausted in a drainage ditch, he in her lap, the skin of his face stretched so tight that it shone in the rain. His stomach bulged with hunger, his feet were swollen and his arms seemed no thicker than my thumbs. She held his face with one hand and in the palm of the other, a small mound of boiled rice which she tried to funnel into his mouth, turning his chin with her fingers to make him chew. He stared at her wide-eyed. Finally, he swallowed, convulsed and died. For a little while longer she held him, watching. Then she dropped him between her knees and covered him in the yellow mud with her feet.

Or maybe it was Saigon, in April 1975, in those final days of the war. We were witnessing a great tragedy, suffering on a scale none of us had ever seen before, political deceit of a kind that made decent men spit at their flag and turn their backs on the monuments to the dead. The Communist Vietnamese army was about to launch its final offensive to take the southern capital of Saigon and the land was emptying as it advanced. A million and more refugees were on the move, searching for safe refuge where they knew there was none any more, not really believing there was sanctuary ahead but knowing only that they were terrified of what was following behind them. In those last days, they had run out of places to run to.

All roads led to Saigon and in the city hysteria was rampant which the Americans did their best to aggravate by their own lies and incompetence. That encouraged international aid and Church agencies to panic and they began to evacuate babies and small children, filling a flight a day, 200 children a time, some still suckling. The evacuation was manna to us journalists who had been living on a diet of death and despair for so long. Now there was a new headline to share: 'CHILDREN OF WAR ON MERCY FLIGHTS TO FREEDOM', and to no one's surprise, newspaper and television news editors back home were enthralled. But then so were we all and many of us made a note of a child's registration number, its flight details and destination and the agency looking after it, promising, as I did, that when we finally made it home, we would seek them out and adopt one for ourselves. Somewhere in the *Daily Mail*'s picture library is a photograph of myself carrying a baby to a plane bound for Britain. I telephoned my wife Diana and she said I should smuggle one home myself – nothing would have been impossible in those final days of chaos and collapse.

The last children to be evacuated out of Saigon's Ton Son Nhut airport left aboard a giant American Air Force transporter, over 350 small children, babies and their keepers, a mass of tiny expectant and frightened faces, ready for the New World and the eager families waiting there to adopt them. But as the enormous Starlifter lumbered into the sky over Saigon, its wheels had barely left the tarmac when it turned over in the air, hit the ground and exploded, the cockpit breaking off from the fuselage and the fuselage from the wings and the four engines spinning across the runway on fire. The heat was intense but as we got closer we saw the fire-fighters picking out the tiny bodies from the debris and piling them in mounds like so much waste.

Thursday, 16 July. I had scribbled in my diary as if to make it irrevocable: 'I shall take a child out of Sarajevo when I leave. Check orphanage about little girl Natasha!' A decision had been made and that was that! But in keeping with a habit of my profession, that you need only say something for it to be true, I had overlooked a rather crucial point; would the orphanage allow Natasha to leave and did she want to go with a complete stranger?

That evening I persuaded Jacko, against his better judgement, to take me back up to the Ljubica Ivezic orphanage, a dangerous journey at dusk through the hills, when the Serb gunners began to adjust their sights on the city in readiness for their night's deadly employment. The streets were empty, the city's people already back in their attics or their cellars to hide the night away in darkness and much fear. Only the occasional blue and white police car sped by and lorries filled with soldiers off to patrol their front lines, to dodge the sniper's bullet and pray that tonight, for once, the shells would land further up the road. But the bearded, dirty, dispirited and hungry men knew there would be empty seats on the lorry home in the morning. There always were.

'Why Natasha?' Mrs Zoric was not as surprised as I had expected. She had left her evening meal to see me and she was followed into the room by the matron and a halfwit, a dirty, lanky boy with a scarred, acned face who hovered behind the director and giggled whenever she spoke.

'Why Natasha, Mr Michael?'

I explained there were other children in her care I could choose if she thought Natasha was not the right choice or if she felt another boy or girl had a greater priority. I would leave it to her to decide, assuming I had her agreement and support.

She smiled, but then tears came into her eyes again and she said something quietly to Jacko in their language and for once Jacko looked sad too.

'But why Natasha?' she asked again.

I shrugged. Why do you select one among so many? Why is one face remembered above the rest?

'She shines,' I said.

Mrs Zoric did not understand but Jacko explained and she and the matron laughed and the halfwit convulsed himself.

I went on: 'She doesn't seem to belong here.'

'None of them belong here.'

'She seems different to me.'

'She will be the same in the end. They are all the same. The boys become thieves and the girls prostitutes and that is as certain as the day they came here.'

'I have a nice house in England. I have a wife and two sons. I have been married a long time. I have a good home.' I heard myself pleading and felt embarrassed. I had brought photographs of my family, my house, my dogs, and I laid them out on the table as if they were credentials. But Mrs Zoric held up her hand.

'Mr Michael . . . you're not taking me to England.' She said something aside to Jacko and again they laughed together. He winked at me and I guessed the meaning. I felt encouraged. At least we were still talking as if my proposal made some sense.

She came and stood closer. 'In the past, before the war, some of my children did go away in the summer holidays to family or friends, it was usually a grandmother . . . it helped us and sometimes it helped them, once or twice it even led to fostering. A few – three or four – have left that way, not many, but orphans are not wanted in this country, especially if a baby is illegitimate. Then the mother's own family disown it and her too if she clings to it, families are very strict, even now. That is why our cellar is full of babies. The churches do not want them and the Communists considered them dirty, an insult to the State, a stain, can you understand?'

She came to me and held my hand in both of hers. 'You want to take this child out of Bosnia and in normal times you could not. But these are not normal times. My children are in danger and every day I am working to find a way to get them out . . . anywhere, to anyone who will look after them. I do not care where they go as long as they are safe, where there are no shells and no bombing, away from Sarajevo. So it is strange that you should come like this and ask me. It is such a strange thing to happen.'

She repeated her last words again, then paused and let go my hand. The halfwit nuzzled her shoulder and she turned and put her arm around him and wiped his mouth clean. No one spoke and in the silence of the room, the Serb guns echoed so much louder and closer. Jacko, the Serb, stood on his own in the corner, nodding his head ever so slightly, looking at the window, an involuntary witness to all the misery and sadness his own people had created.

At last Mrs Zoric spoke. 'I can only agree to you taking Natasha away on condition it is for a holiday and that you will bring her back here when the new school term begins in the autumn, or when the war ends, whichever is the sooner.' How matter-of-fact she made it seem, a string of conditions as if I was borrowing a bicycle for the summer! Whichever is the sooner, she said, but did she really believe, knowing what she knew and guessing at what was still to come, that the war would be over by the autumn? Did she mean this year or next? And a new school term? In what school and where in this devastated city? When the last shell had landed and the warmongers were finally persuaded by the peacebrokers to sign their place into the history books, what kind of Bosnia would I return little Natasha to? Would there still be a Bosnia?

'Will you ask her, Mrs Zoric?'

'I will go now and tell her what you say.'

She spoke briefly to Jacko and he translated: 'She says you should wait alone. I shall go to the car,' which seemed to me the oddest thing.

'She wants to know how long she will stay – so she knows how much love she must give.'
Natasha with Max, in the garden, Grayswood, May 1993.

Above: 'One by one we touched each other's glass and welcomed our new companion.' Natasha with cameraman Jon Martin (right) and Russ Padwick (left) at Split, 19 July 1992.

Left: 'Now she has prepared herself to be the surrogate mother to the little stranger.' Diana in the garden with Natasha, summer 1993.

'Once the novelty had worn off, she became just another pupil with a funny accent.' Natasha's first day at St Bartholomew's School, September 1992.

'She said it was her "Bestest Day" and we hardly needed telling.' Natasha's tenth birthday and her first ever party and her first ever candles and cake, October 1992.

Left: 'Who would recognize the war-waif now – registered orphan 388 of no great expectations.' I teach her cricket – Grayswood, September 1992.

Below: 'Long after her first anniversary she had pushed away the ghosts of Sarajevo's yesteryears.' Learning to swim with Max, Grayswood, September 1992. Within a week Natasha could swim a length.

I was left with the halfwit. He stood in the corner of the room, half in light, one eye closed, the other wide and unblinking, half a smile, half a scowl, brave for an instant, moving into the lamp's glare, then scurrying back into his corner, hiding from me and all the misery around us. The window was crisscrossed with sticky tape but I could see the hills and mountains surrounding Sarajevo. Across the scorched and blackened tiled rooftops of the old quarter, beyond the mosque's dome and minarets, were the forests where the Serbs had dug in with their guns, the guns that had shattered this city and all but silenced its people. They had hit the orphanage again and blown a hole in the side of the nursery, which was why the older children were living in the cellar with the babies. Natasha was there now. On the far side of the city, smoke was rising as straight and as black as from a chimney. Something was always burning there and someone always dying. Maybe a Serb sniper, seeing my shadow in the light, was even at that moment training his telescopic sights on this window. I could imagine a mortar being pushed through the mud somewhere in the cover of those trees: soon there would be another flash and a thousand searing fragments and another bout of dying. It was a city waiting to die and the world was watching. And there I sat, a stranger in Sarajevo, come to take away a little orphan girl.

Finally, after nearly half an hour, they came back and she was with them, unsmiling, holding their hands tightly, not looking at me. I assumed the worst. They had been away much longer than it was ever necessary to have her answer a simple yes or no.

'Yes, Mr Michael,' said Mrs Zoric, 'she will come with you to England for a holiday. But she only asks how long it will be for. You understand? She wants to know how much love she must give.'

I heard the familiar rumble outside and saw flashes of light in the darkening sky, the beginning of the night's bombardment. Somebody brought coffee and the four of us sat down, the halfwit hovering. I broke open a bar of chocolate and spread out my photographs on the table for her to see. Then they told me Natasha's story.

Acting on impulse is not the same as acting in haste. But haste was the keyword now. I was near the end of my three-week assignment and a replacement crew and reporter were due to arrive in Sarajevo that coming Saturday on an RAF relief flight. Jon, Russ and myself had to be at the airport to take the returning plane out, that was how the change-overs were done. So I had two days left to make arrangements if Natasha was to come with us.

General Lewis Mackenzie had no choice but to say no. I had no choice but to ask. As the Canadian Commander of the UN Peacekeeping Force in Sarajevo, and the best ambassador Canada ever had. He was in overall charge of the relief operation. In confidence, I told him what I proposed to do and asked him if he would allow Natasha to accompany me and the crew aboard Saturday's flight to Zagreb in Croatia. Getting her to England from there would then be my problem.

The General was known as a kind, fair and practical man. He was also under enormous pressure from many of the world's charities to fly children out of the city on the empty returning relief flights, something we had ourselves highlighted in our recent reports from Sarajevo. As it happened, it was also something he privately admitted he was keen to do. He was a father, he said, and would give his right arm to save the children. 'I'd pack them in from dawn to dusk, given the chance,' was how he put it to me. But without adequate protection he said, 'The idea of taking busloads of children and sick out to the airport is really quite bizarre. There's no way we want a firefight with refugees or whatever along that road. We simply do not have the firepower to provide them that protection.'

As for taking one child out, he said, one privileged little child who had caught the eye of a British television correspondent, the answer was no . . . absolutely no! Once it became known, as it would, he would have people queueing up all the way from the city centre, many of them probably a great deal more deserving. If he did it for one, he asked, then why not for all? He shook my hand and wished me luck and then got on with the more pressing business of Sarajevo's bigger problems.

One down, one to go and then what? I went to the organizer of the UNHCR, the UN High Commission for Refugees. Their food convoys entered the besieged city whenever the Serbs allowed them through and the lorries then left empty. Would he allow me and Natasha to leave on the next one? Again I knew his answer before I had finished my question but all options, however forlorn, had to be tried. Less patient than General Mackenzie and more direct, he stopped just short of calling me a dangerous fool. How could his organization be compromised in such a way? he asked. Did I know what I was asking of him? Did I appreciate the risks? What if one of a dozen Serb road-blocks searched the convoy, as they often did, and found Natasha? What would they do to her? Would I see her again? I was behaving irresponsibly, recklessly. Did I really expect to smuggle a girl of nine out of Sarajevo to England as if she were a teddy bear? He ended: 'Your motive is admirable, it is for the best possible reason. But have you really thought it through at both ends and the dangerous bit in the middle?'

I had not. It was a sombre conversation, an immensely depressing cautionary tale. How easy it had been to make too much of an assumption, to express it and therefore believe it and by believing make it happen. I had not thought my decision through, but then if I had, perhaps I would not have made the decision at all. If I could not find a way out for both of us, however, what then? Did I leave without Natasha, without telling her, without an explanation to Mrs Zoric? Assuming I had the courage to face them, what would I say, what would my excuse be? That it was a great idea but there were transport problems? That it could not be helped and maybe next time we could try again? That I had been silly, impulsive, infantile and should have arranged the way out before inviting her to leave?

And what then? Give her a box of chocolates as compensation?

All that Thursday night I sat watching the war sky over Sarajevo, following the arc of tracer rounds from Muslim gunners to Serbs and back again, hearing the great crashes as shells pushed houses apart, the soft whistle of shells passing overhead and the whine of the snipers' bullets. They were reminders of the closeness of the dying city and they helped concentrate my mind.

Given that I could not take Natasha out, I had only one honourable option: to stay behind until I could. In the course of that uneasy night I had made that decision at least. But my reason for staying must remain a secret. Outside of the orphanage, only three people knew of my plan, but if it became known to the press in Sarajevo and in London, the publicity would stymie everything. It would mean a string of lies to ITN London and in turn, to my wife Diana, because if I did not catch the Saturday flight with the crew, both would need an explanation and a faulty alarm clock would not do!

I had not told Diana of my decision even though I had access to both ITN's and CNN's satellite telephones. I was afraid she would reject the whole idea as absurd – after all, she was at the receiving end, it was she who would have to cope with the problems and traumas Natasha was bound to carry to England with her. What had the UN man said? Have you thought it through at *both* ends?

The night magnified the problems and made them all seem unsolvable. Only twenty-four hours before I had embarked on such a simple crusade, giving a stranger's promise to a little girl who had held his pictures of England in her hands and had smiled as he spoke his stranger's words. She would be awake now, listening to the same bombardment, so much closer to her now, watching the same white flashes in the black sky and believing she was seeing the last of them because she was going away to England, to a house in a place called Surrey and a little white dog called Max . . . until the new school term, until the war was over. Whichever was the sooner.

Who was she, this tiny thing who in less than a minute's meeting had made me a casualty of her war? How had she enticed an ageing correspondent who had time and again publicly declared that the next war would be his last, to postpone his departure from this one so readily? She was not, as I had suspected, a war orphan, that is, she had not lost her parents because of it. She had been dumped at the orphanage when she was five months old by an unmarried mother shamed into abandoning her baby by a strict family in an unforgiving, patriarchal, Communist society. Her father was not known, that at least is what the records stated. Her mother, whose name was Milica, worked for a large Sarajevo building company and she travelled with it on frequent foreign contracts to the Soviet Union and Iran. According to the orphanage records, Milica did not visit Natasha again until she was eight years old. The child welfare officer, who must have been present at their meetings wrote: 'The emotional bond between Natasha and her mother did not show warm relations. The child is not happy to see her.'

The original registration book marking the baby girl's arrival at the orphanage on 24 March 1983 gives her number as 388 and her name as Jelena, which means 'deer'. But as the child grew up, knowing who she was and why she was where she was, she rejected the name her mother had given her and called herself Natasha instead.

Gradually, as the night went on, the noise and sound of war receded until even the distant guns on the mountains were still. The gunners had grown tired and bored and had gone to bed. The war-makers of Sarajevo invariably began their shelling at dusk and reached a busy crescendo around midnight, then slowly lost interest so that by around three in the morning it was all over for another night. There were those who believed this had nothing to do with military strategy and everything to do with drinking habits, that both sides filled themselves with plum brandy and nicotine until they reached saturation point about midday. Then they slept it off until the sun went down and it was time to begin the bombardment all over again.

Except, that is, on Saturdays and Sundays when the shelling was more intensive and more accurate and casualties soared. Nobody really discovered how or why, though there was a story that Serb regular army gunners were sent to Sarajevo from Belgrade at weekends for artillery and mortar practice. Perhaps promotion depended on a high target count. Whoever they were, they did their bit to help send this once great city to its death.

I could hear piano music, Gershwin. Another nocturnal was playing the grand piano amidst the wreckage on the second floor. It was four o'clock and there seemed more movement below than usual at this time of the morning. Perhaps somebody new had arrived, but what brave souls had travelled through the night to Sarajevo? I got up and pulled the mattress from the hole where the window had been. It was black out there, quite still, and a breeze from the south carried the smell of burning. I prepared an earlier than usual breakfast – bottled water and what was left of a tin of corned beef. Later, when they were boiling water downstairs, I would make my own tea, the first and most necessary ritual of the day. I went nowhere beyond Dover without my teabags and I tied a mental knot to remember to ask the replacement crew to bring in more, now that I had made up my mind to stay longer here.

It began to get light a little after five, so, washed and shaved and partly fed, I went out into the corridors to see who had been daring enough to cross no man's land at such an hour. Four people were standing at the bar drinking tiny cups of Turkish coffee, enveloped in a smog that smelt unmistakably of French cigarettes. At the main door of the hotel, parked where none of us had ever dared park because of the snipers, was a white Landrover with the words 'EQUILIBRE. L'ENTREPRISE HUMANITAIRE' emblazoned across its doors. Other curious journalists joined the newcomers and I squeezed in among them. Alain Michel introduced himself as the leader of the group; he was accompanied by a diminutive blonde girl, Dany Héricourt, who spoke the most perfect English because, as she explained with a smile, she had the most perfect English mother.

Dany briefed us. 'We are bringing in food and medicines in a fourteen-lorry convoy. They'll be here today and if all the unloading goes well we aim to leave again on Saturday. We have coaches coming in too and we shall be taking children out to Split on the Croatian coast. The Italian government will fly them on to Milan, where it is arranging foster homes for them.'

I tried not to sound too excited. 'What children . . . how many . . . where from?'

'All who want to come and as many as we can carry,' she said. 'We are being helped by an agency here . . . it calls itself the First Children's Embassy. They will give us the lists. It could be a dangerous journey, no one has tried it before with children and we're asking for UN protection at least until we are beyond the Serb lines.'

And that is how it happened. Suddenly, out of the early morning darkness, an escape route was announced. All the while I had been fretting, there was a plan already in motion, a plan that with a little bit of guile, could include Natasha and me. I was already working on it!

'Dany,' I said, introducing myself, 'I would be fascinated to cover this convoy of yours for British television, to come with you. It would make a wonderful story . . . you the Pied Piper taking the children over the mountains to the sea.' Then I went and found boiling water and I made her tea.

CHAPTER FOUR

T he list was the thing and Natasha had to be on it. Only the First Children's Embassy could add her name, so that was where I spent most of that Friday morning. I met Lajla Kozemjakin, who was one of the principals in an organization of Muslims, Serbs and Croats with one thing in common; they were all Bosnian with a shared concern to save the children of Sarajevo from a siege they knew would get progressively worse. Within a few months, Lajla said, the October winds would come and after them the snow blizzards. 'The winter will kill,' she said. 'If the world has not helped us by then, without food, without fuel, without heat, too many of our children will die. Already people are cutting down trees to stock up for their stoves . . . already, and it is only July. That is how certain we are that the siege will go beyond Christmas.'

I interviewed her and she pleaded on camera for the UN to make their empty aircraft available to take out the children and the sick. She wept when I reminded her that General Mackenzie had already given a definitive 'No'. She said they already had over 2000 names but once they had managed to get the first convoy safely out she expected a stampede . . . there were over 30,000 children under the age of fourteen in the city. The first to go would be those who had no families to protect them, mostly orphans. Then it would be a matter of first come, first away. 'Every mother will want her child to go,' she said, 'it will be so much easier to survive alone. Then one day perhaps they will come back to Sarajevo and we will have families again.'

Lajla wrote Natasha's name into the list. I had only to ask her once, but she did not say if some other child had been scratched off, nor did I have the nerve to ask her. Nothing is entirely selfless and if I felt guilt at that moment, I soon forgot it in the rush to get things done.

Natasha was now assured a seat on the Pied Piper's convoy, so now it was time to persuade ITN London that I and the crew should go too, that the story was worth the hassle the decision would cause with the British Ministry of Defence who regulated the RAF flights into Sarajevo. It was Ministry policy that a television crew would only be given a flight in on a Hercules if a television crew came out on the return flight. Ministry decisions seldom have anything to do with common sense and the rule puzzled us all, but in true bureaucratic fashion no one in Whitehall ever thought it warranted an explanation.

That afternoon via the satellite telephone link, my foreign editor told me he did think the hassle worthwhile; this was after all the very first children's convoy out and we would be the only television crew with it. Piece by piece, my complicated jigsaw was coming together.

Later that day I went to the orphanage for the last time to say goodbye to Mrs Zoric and get from her a vital piece of paper giving me written authority to take Natasha away. It was already waiting:

> At the personal request of Michael Nicholson of Surrey, England, passport B466188. through the intervention of the First Children's Embassy and with the agreement of the Children's Home 'Ljubica Ivezic' and the agreement of Natasha Mihaljcic, minor, it is agreed that she stay temporarily in the home of Mr Nicholson, either during the summer holiday until the start of the new school year, or until the end of the war in the Republic of Bosnia, or to the end of immediate war threats in the area around the city of Sarajevo. The child Natasha is taken from the Home in a good state of health and Mr Nicholson is taking full responsibility for her care and protection

It was signed and dated 18 July the following day.

The convoy was due to leave the next day, Saturday, but

shortly after I left the orphanage, we were told it might not. Mick Magnussan, the UN official acting as go-between, was trying to negotiate a one-hour ceasefire to allow the convoy to pass across the front lines. Now he was no longer certain that an agreement he had made with the commanders of all three warring sides would be obeyed at street-fighter level. He knew, as we all did, that a smiling officer in a dapper uniform can agree one thing, but it is altogether different when you are faced by a road-block of ragged, bearded red-eyed Chetniks – the Serb irregulars – smelling of brandy, pushing the barrel of their gun into your stomach. Magnussan realized the dangers and envisaged the bitter recriminations if any child was killed or wounded in a convoy that had been sanctioned by the UN. He had also been asked to provide armoured car escorts out of the city for 15 miles to the first Croatian road-block at Kiseljak, safely beyond the dangerous Serb lines. But under the UN mandate, as it was then, he was obliged not to put his soldiers at risk. Quite properly, he was not prepared to gamble on a fire-fight with his men in the middle.

All that evening we waited and every hour I telephoned Magnussan's office for news. There was none. Thirty parents had already brought their children to the football stadium, Saturday's pick-up point, to camp there, afraid that any new outburst of fighting nearby might prevent them from reaching it in the morning. In many homes that night across the city, children, confused with excitement and fear, would have their little bags already packed for the early start on their journey over the mountains to the sea and who knew what beyond. For certain, I knew one of them.

Silhouetted in candlelight on the ground floor of the wrecked Holiday Inn, Alain Michel and Dany Héricourt sat waiting under their Gauloise cloud, their small army of volunteer drivers sitting in groups around them, talking, writing, waiting. They were no strangers to risk but tomorrow's would be altogether different – the stakes would be higher, the odds as always unfavourable. They had been told by the UN to wait for at least some guarantee of safety, and considering who it was they would be carrying, wait they would.

It would have been sensible, despite the late hour, to have boiled water and used the last of my teabags. Whisky could only make things worse tomorrow, if tomorrow was to be the travelling day. But good sense and bad times do not always sit easily together, and who would drink tea at a time like this? So the bottle I had saved for our final night was opened and it did the ceremonial round, passing from hand to grubby hand, each raised in turn with a salute, until it was empty.

Then, with the perfect timing that might win applause on stage, Dany's radio telephone buzzed. There was silence. Then Dany gave a great whoop and shouted in French, and the drivers cheered. Magnussan had given the green light, the Serbs had agreed to let them pass. We would leave the UN headquarters on the airport road, escorted by armoured cars flying the famous blue flag, tomorrow at ten sharp. We were on our way!

Saturday, 18 July. The incessant shelling, the remorseless sniper fire and now the prospect of a winter under siege, made the city despair; each day bleaker than the day before, with the prospect of tomorrow bleaker still. Getting the children out to safety had become everybody's imperative, even if it meant handing them to strangers who would take them to who knew where, for who knew how long. Sarajevo might be destroyed but a generation must be saved to rebuild it.

Equilibre's coaches arrived at the stadium at first light and families immediately surrounded them, little groups huddled together, some fathers but mostly only mothers, fussing about their children, tying a belt tighter, pulling a sock higher, tidying a headscarf, rechecking the contents of little rucksacks and carrier bags . . . leaving their goodbyes until the very last moment. And all the time looking to the mountains, to the Serb gunners who were certainly watching them.

Soon it was time to go, time to hug and kiss and join the

queue. Names were ticked off the list and a dozen helping hands guided children to their seats, tearful children taken from tearful mothers who kissed the window that separated them, mothers who perhaps only then understood what it was they were doing, suddenly uncertain and afraid they would never see their child again, as many would not. But they knew that to love their children was to save them and to save them was to lose them. It was a mother's sacrifice: mine had done the same, along with countless others to save their sons and daughters from Hitler's blitz. A label had been tied around my neck like any piece of baggage, I was given a gas mask in a cardboard box and sandwiches in an Oxo tin, and after a wet-faced hug it was off to the scary unknown, to a family I had never met, in a place I had never heard of. In that instant a mother was lost in a platform of Paddington station steam, a mother on her way back to the black-outs and the air-raid shelter under the stairs to wait for another night of the Luftwaffe's incendiaries . . . childless, alone and without hope.

How the children of Sarajevo cried as we pulled out of the stadium, dazed by the abruptness of it all, wondering why, having survived so much for so long, they had been abandoned by the only people who had loved and protected them. And how brave the older ones were, like thirteen-year-old Danijela, who sat with two little boys on her knees leading the singing. At the back of the coach, in seat number 28, a little girl sat watching. She had seen the others kiss and cry their goodbyes but she had no one to kiss and no reason to cry. Natasha was leaving Sarajevo and its war, and that morning she was happy. As she was to tell much, much later, she had already promised herself she would not return until she was much, much older. She knew that none of the other children had any idea where they were going or who they were going to. But she did, she had seen the stranger's photographs. She was going to England and she hoped it would be for a long time, because then she could give her love as she had never been able to before. And perhaps, for the first time in her life, she might be loved in return.

The UN armoured cars at the head of the convoy led us through parts of Sarajevo I had not seen before, where no journalist or cameraman would ever have dared venture, where any movement of man or machine would have provoked a massive and immediate bombardment. Slowly we drove along Sniper's Alley, under the flyover and left through the twisting chicane of burnt-out lorries, past an upturned tank and over the railway line. There was a pile of bloated and rotting bodies by the blown-up signal box, heaped together as if waiting collection, their faces puffed up, the skin so tight they looked as if they were about to burst. We could smell their stench as we passed. The men who had promised us safe passage had kept their word, and only at the final Serb road-block did they come aboard, cursing at us, spitting phlegm at the windows, pushing the children, slapping little frightened faces when they did not move fast enough or answer their bawling questions quickly. They emptied bags and boxes, tipping them up with the end of their rifle barrels, searching for weapons, sweeping a dagger or a bayonet under the seats looking for any escaping Muslim fighter. The few women in the coach held their breath, convinced the Serbs would haul the children off and keep them hostage. But then they were gone and they waved their driver on.

The devastation was appalling. It was like something we remembered watching in wartime newsreels of defeated Germany. Europe had seen nothing like it since. Mile after mile of the city had been all but erased, houses gutted or perforated by gunfire, factories shelled into mounds of twisted metal, thirty-storey office blocks burnt out so completely that only the skeletal steel framework was evidence they had ever existed. What had been an industrial complex had become a geometrical nightmare of acres of girders twisted into complicated triangles and trapezoids sprouting from pyramids of rubble that had once been the fillings in between. In the sprawl of brick and rubble, what had once been pleasant, leafy suburbs had lost their contours as if they had never existed, and long avenues of trees had been torn and shredded. Railway lines destroyed by mines had erupted into giant iron circles, street-light pylons had fallen across each other, creating a lattice-work, burying the rusty shells of burnt-out cars and lorries beneath them. All this had been accomplished in only four months. But then, 2500 shells had been landing on some days, such was the intensity of the bombardment, and there were over 6000 dead, such was the thoroughness of the killing.

We passed a madman. He was black with dirt, dressed only in a waistcoat and shorts, dancing, prancing in a garden that might once have been his, in front of a shell of a house that could have been his home. His bare feet were bloody from the glass splinters and bricks and when he saw the children he pulled his mouth wide with his fingers and rolled his eyes. We slowed to pass into a narrow alley and he came running after us, pounding the side of the coach with his fists. The children laughed and waved, not understanding, and when I looked back, he was standing quite still in the middle of the debris, fingers in his mouth again with tears streaming down his filthy face. It was my last image of Sarajevo that day.

Kiseljak, 15 miles from Sarajevo, was the first Croatian road-block and for us it meant safety, even though it was where our UN armed escorts left us. From now on the convoy was on its own with only Alain and Dany to guide us through to Split. We could not go the quick and easy way along the main road to Mostar because there was intensive fighting there too. The secondary road was also unusable as all its bridges had been blown up. So our Pied Pipers decided to navigate us through the maze of mountain tracks, some of them hardly wider than the lorries' and coaches' wheels, tracks that at one moment were muddy and slippery from spring water and as dry and as cracked as a desert the next.

The plan was to get to a plateau, thousands of feet up, and

spend the night there. Dany knew of a lake where the children could wash and swim, and the prospect encouraged us. But very quickly it became clear we would not get far that day. The tracks crumbled with the vehicles' weight and some of the turns were so narrow and sharp that it often took the drivers an hour and more to manoeuvre their giant articulated lorries through them. At times the main convoy had to wait to allow one lorry at a time to climb a steep slippery pass on its own in case it lost power or its grip and slid back. One came close to toppling over, its front off-side wheel spinning over the edge.

It was an anxious journey, not only because of the sheer drop thousands of feet to the valley below but because of our constant preoccupation with the sounds of war not so far away, the boom of guns and the occasional bursts of machine-gun fire echoing across the vast pine forests. We had a clear view from one mountain ridge to another, and could sometimes even see the track we were following, winding its way up miles ahead. But there was no comfort in the sight as there was no way of knowing how close the Serbs were or where they were moving to. What had been Croat territory yesterday and declared safe for us, might easily have changed hands overnight. The Serb Chetniks had a well-documented reputation as wanton, drunken killers and rapists and many of us had seen something of their work in Vukovar and elsewhere, mass graves filled with the bodies of those they had executed for pleasure or spite. They were the most feared of all the fighters in this terrible war and it would have been so easy for them to ambush us and take whatever they wanted, our food, the lorries, the women, the children.

The higher we drove deeper into those black forests, the more uncertain we all became. And the night still lay ahead. The children knew nothing of this, of course. Once we were away from the towns and the soldiers and into the countryside, the coaches had become a babble of happy noise. Tears had long dried and the sad goodbyes, like Sarajevo itself, had already been forgotten. Now the talk was of the mountains and the sea and there was enormous excitement when they were told that they would be travelling from Split to Italy on a boat. How quickly the thrill of the future was pushing away the past!

Throughout, I kept watch on Natasha. Her escape was our secret and she was enjoying the intrigue. She had quickly lost her shyness and every so often, when she knew no one was looking, she gave me silent signals. I slipped her a bar of chocolate which, to my pleasure, she broke into many pieces and shared out. I had not told my camera crew Jon and Russ what I intended, that once in Split, the children would go one way and she another, though where to and how, I had still to work out. I could stay with the children and go over on the ferry to Italy, then hire a car in Brindisi and fly from Rome to London. But I knew nothing of the Italian government's arrangements for the children at the other end, nor was I confident I could bluff my way past Italian Immigration. Perhaps it would be better to stay in a country at war, where I could take advantage of the war's confusion. It might be wiser to take the day-long drive from Split to Zagreb and make the run there, then if things went wrong Natasha was still in her own country.

As we had feared, we arrived at the plateau with the sun already down, too late and too cold for the children to wash or paddle in the lake. To keep warm and busy, they were told to gather wood and within ten minutes we had blazing bonfires and they sat around them eating slices of bread and cheese, their faces ruddy with the heat. It was Guy Fawkes Night without the fireworks. But those other deadly pyrotechnics were not so far off, north of us now, and every few minutes the sky beyond the plateau's edge glowed red, and tiny white flashes punctured the dark blue sky. The children stopped their chatter and listened to the bombardment of Mostar, the once beautiful regional capital with its prairie of vineyards, only 12 miles away.

It was to be the children's last image of the war. Soon the fires had burned themselves out and they were shivering again, so Alain and Dany decided not to wait but to carry on through the night and stop at dawn in the warmer valleys below. The children slept all through that dark and dangerous descent, the drivers spinning their steering wheels left and right, hour after hour, peering into the yellow light of their headlamps until their eyes as well as their arms ached. By the time we reached the flat valley floor they had been driving for over eighteen hours with just that one brief rest. They were extraordinary men who made no boast of what they were doing, and after that journey, many of them would return again and again with supplies to keep the hungry of Sarajevo from starving.

It was a beautiful dawn and the sun was already big and bright by the time the coaches stopped and the children ran out to play in the fields. For all of them, these were the first fields they had seen in over four months; for some, the first they had ever seen. Villagers came out from their warm kitchens, curious at the sudden invasion, wondering how we had arrived and why these tired and unwashed children should find the early morning ablutions of cattle and calves so amusing.

Natasha and other girls were splashing their faces in a stream, while Jon, Russ and I had breakfast in the village bar. Over a brandy and beer I told them what I intended to do. They wanted to help, as I knew they would, but I made them promise they would not involve themselves, to save ITN any public embarrassment should things go wrong. It was a promise they had quickly to undo.

We came out from the bar to find a BBC camera crew filming. Having been alerted by Martin Bell in Sarajevo and told of our probable route, they had come from Split to meet us and intended sending the story by satellite to London in time for their midday news. That meant I would have to follow suit, leave the convoy and hitch a lift back to Split to edit and feed my story. Jon and Russ, far from being interested spectators, had now to keep watch on Natasha and, once arrived in Split, take her with them. Lajla Kozemjakin agreed and gave her promise to arrange the handover discreetly, because since the BBC knew of the convoy, almost certainly other press would be waiting in Split for its arrival and there would be a hue and cry if Natasha was seen disappearing with a camera crew.

Lajla kept her word and the plan worked. I sent my report via the European Broadcasting satellite for ITN's Sunday lunchtime news and by the time I had reached the docks, the children were boarding the ferry bound for Italy and Natasha was already on her way with the crew to our hotel.

That evening, we stood on the balcony overlooking the Adriatic Sea, watching a glorious Dalmatian sunset, three of us sipping champagne, the fourth Coca-Cola, exhausted but safely arrived and very content. One by one we touched each other's glass and I welcomed our new companion, calling her my Bosnian princess, which seemed to please her. Then we sat and ate and toasted our good fortune until it was dark. I wrapped Natasha in a blanket and soon she was fast asleep on the couch. She would have slept earlier but she had sat for more than an hour, fascinated by the sea she had never seen before and by the moon's reflections on it. As she settled down, she taught me a new word in her language: 'privati'. She was very insistent about it, repeating it and using her hands until I understood what she wanted. Tomorrow, I promised her, we would go swimming so that she could touch the sea for the very first time in her life.

Once Jon and Russ had gone to sleep, I telephoned Diana. I had forgotten how late it was and she too had been asleep, so that what followed must have made her wonder afterwards if she had simply dreamed it all. 'Do you remember,' I began, 'when I was in Saigon all those years ago and those hundreds of orphan babies were being flown out? . . . You saw it on television. You said I should bring one home to you. Do you remember saying that our house was big enough and we had the money and we should give some poor child a chance?' There were sleepy mumbles from the Surrey end of the line. I tried not to sound too triumphant. 'Well, I've just brought one out of Sarajevo.'

'A Vietnamese baby?' There was need for a little patience.

'No, Diana . . . Sarajevo is in Bosnia . . . that's where I've been for the past fortnight. I've got a little Bosnian girl. She's nine. She's an orphan and she's great! You'll love her.' I paused, waiting for a response, but there was none.

I went on, 'There could be a problem. I've still got to get her out of the country.' I should not have said this.

'Why the problem?' she asked, suddenly alert. But it was far too late to explain to a tired wife the next day's Gordian knot or how I hoped to untie it. Nor was this the hour to tell her that the next call from me might be from a Croatian prison. So in my usual way when confronted with a difficult situation, I sidestepped it. I told her that there were still a few formalities to be completed, a few hands to be greased, and that I would ring her once we had landed at Heathrow and cleared British Immigration. In the morning she should make up a bed for her new lodger because we would be home for lunch with a story to tell.

I wished her goodnight but Diana, as she told me later, did not sleep any more that night. Instead she went downstairs to the pantry, poured herself a very large Scotch and pondered the benefits and otherwise of her life's association with me!

Now began the masquerade. Natasha was no longer an orphan from Sarajevo. If we were to go together to England she had to become my daughter, quickly and convincingly. She had left the orphanage wearing a grubby blouse, a pair of black shorts and sandals. Inside her miniature cardboard suitcase was a comb, a toothbrush and half a towel. So we began our shopping spree together to start the process to Anglicize her. I bought her shampoo and she washed and brushed her hair until it shone. I bought her a Mickey Mouse T-shirt and a teddy bear and a canvas bag with 'HI EVERYBODY!' gaudily printed on it in the hope that no one would be in any doubt what language she spoke.

But that morning it failed the first test. The Croat driver taking the four of us to Zagreb realized immediately that she was Bosnian and quickly established that she was from Sarajevo. I wondered just how much of his questioning was curiosity and how much suspicion, remembering that until only recently this had been a Communist state with all its associated trickery and deception. Informers to the secret police had earned a very profitable living here. Might he contact the police once we had arrived in Zagreb? Three Englishmen with a Bosnian child were unusual enough to warrant reporting. Inventing an excuse, I moved Natasha out of conversation range to the back seat, to sit between Jon and Russ, and told the driver that we had brought her from Sarajevo to stay with her grandmother in Zagreb. A humanitarian gesture, I said humbly. He seemed satisfied but I knew it might take a 100-dollar bonus at the end of our drive to keep him that way.

We followed the road along that magnificent coast until we reached Zadar but then, instead of turning inland to cross the Velebitski Gorge by the Maslenica Bridge, we were stopped at a military road-block and sent left, up a long narrow peninsula to Pog. We were told that the bridge, which was almost half a mile across, had been blown up by the Serbs as they advanced from their enclave in Krijina. It had connected Croatia with its southern Dalmatian coast and its destruction now cut the country in two. We would have to cross on a ferry at a safer point further up the coast and then motor north, still hugging the sea, towards Rijeka. Just south of that city we could at last turn inland, crossing more mountains to Karlovac and finally Zagreb. It would add another five hours to our journey but Natasha minded not a bit and the prospect of a ferry crossing made her forget her travel sickness and her embarrassment at the little plastic bags of vomit we had been depositing at inter- vals along the route.

We arrived in the Croatian capital a little before midnight too exhausted to eat, too tired even for a final celebratory drink. As the crew checked me into the Intercontinental Hotel, I carried a sleeping Natasha to bed. It was a warm night, the window was open, and from it I could see the city, the floodlit opera house and cathedral and beyond them, to the left, the sprawl of the red roofs of Parliament. How cleverly they had illuminated the old quarter; from this distance it looked unreal, like a stupendous painted backdrop on a gigantic stage. Even at this hour people were still about, the wide, tree-lined streets busy with rumbling trams and cars darting between them. How normal it was now, and yet I remembered when I had heard the air-raid sirens and seen Serbian MIG jets bomb the Presidency. I remembered seeing road-blocks where the late-night window-shoppers were now, as men with shotguns and hunting rifles had tried to ambush the federal tanks. Zagreb had survived its war. How far away now in time and distance Sarajevo seemed, a city that might not survive.

A searchlight moved around the cathedral, catching the spire and panning across the clock-face. Soon it would be Tuesday, 21 July, and at eleven o'clock that morning, Croatia Airlines flight 490 would take off for London. I intended both of us to be on it. It was our last, most difficult and perhaps insurmountable hurdle. But if we failed, what then? I would be arrested of course. Trying to smuggle a child out of any country, whatever the circumstances, was a criminal offence. Arrest meant jail for as long as it took the British Ambassador to arrange my release, assuming such was the Foreign Office's pleasure. Arrest would mean the Croatians taking charge of Natasha, Mrs Zoric's written authority would mean nothing here and she would be treated like any other illegal immigrant and sent to a transit hostel until somebody decided what to do with her, whether to send her back to Sarajevo or not. Not for the first time that past week, the night panicked me, as if only after dark were my foolish schemes exposed and all the reasons for not pursuing them explained.

The cathedral bells slowly struck midnight, soft sounds far away, but I closed the window and drew the curtains. Natasha did not stir but nothing should disturb her sleep tonight. She had a hard day ahead, a crucial day that would decide her future one way or another, promising her a start in a new world or condemning her back to the old. Yet we had come so far and we were now so near, it was not possible we would fail. It had been decided.

She stirred, and I tucked the sheet tighter around her. On the writing table was my passport, number B 466188. I opened it and carefully wrote under my name in the columns provided: 'Accompanied by one child, Natasha. Daughter. Born 7.10.82.' Then the final chore before I went to sleep. I washed her shorts and socks and stretched them over the radiator and pressed her new T-shirt under the mattress so that Mickey Mouse would look clean and smart and convincing in the morning.

I had arranged for Jon and Russ to leave the hotel a half-hour ahead of Natasha and me. We would follow separately. They were being driven by the same suspicious man who had brought us from Split and despite my present of a 100-dollar bill on top of his hire charge, I thought it wiser to keep apart for two reasons; first, so that Jon could convince him I had gone to take Natasha to her family outside Zagreb; second, that if I was stopped at the airport, Jon and Russ and ITN should not be implicated. If the worst happened, as far as they and the company were concerned, I had acted alone and secretively. I also thought it a sensible precaution to buy two business-class tickets; the bigger the bluff the more likely I was to succeed, and after all I was, as I would tell the police and Immigration officers, a businessman taking his daughter back to her boarding-school in England. Natasha looked the part and even if she would not pass as an Anglo-Saxon, there must be many Englishmen married to Slavs whose daughters looked very similar. She had strict instructions from me not to speak and, just as important, she was to show off her T-shirt, her teddy bear and the silly 'HI EVERYBODY!' carrier bag. For good measure, I had her carry an armful of day-old British newspapers.

The first ordeal was the police security examination. They searched my bags, I offered my passport, they hardly looked at it, so I went to move on.

They held up their hands. 'Girl passport,' they demanded.

'No, no!' I smiled my broadest. Natasha, taking the hint, did the same. 'She's on mine . . . look, it's here . . . in England we put our children on our passports.' My heart thumped as they flicked the pages. How often had they seen a child's entry before? Had they ever? Did they believe it? They did, and we walked on to the next and final examination.

The two policemen had been older men and at their trade a long time. In front of us now, behind her glass partition, was a young girl with a single gold band on her epaulette, a beginner. I handed over the passport and boarding cards and then, deliberately loudly and purposely gruffly, I told Natasha to pay attention and not to drop the newspapers, chiding her for being so careless. She played the game. She did what she was told and grinned back.

'The little devil travels on my passport,' I said, feigning the exasperation of parents at such times. The bored young girl hardly looked at me or my passport, but she stamped it with a bang and pushed it back across her counter. I held Natasha's hand tight and we walked on, hardly believing we had done it so easily. Ahead was a flight of stairs leading to the Departure Lounge and the Duty Free and gate number 3, the gate for our flight 409. We had made it.

'One moment! Stop!' someone shouted behind us. I turned and froze. Another woman, another immigration officer, older, fatter, with two rings on her grubby grey uniform, came hurrying towards me.

'Passport,' she said, stony-faced, holding out her fat hand, 'and boarding cards.' I handed them to her, suddenly, horribly nauseous with the sensation of déjà vu, remembering scenes like this in so many films . . . caught at the final barrier, turned back at the last fence, found out, here, now, helpless, losing control, a grey uniform, my passport and tickets in her hands. This is how it would end. Natasha stood a few yards behind me, waiting. The newspapers dropped to the floor. I felt like dropping to my knees to join them.

'Stamps . . . no stamps,' the woman spat out, the habit of Communist rudeness hard to break.

'Stamps?' I repeated, bewildered.

'No stamps, no airport tax. You pay 3000 dinars for stamps.'

'Do you take dollars?' I asked sweetly. I would happily have given her gold!

One of the extravagances of business-class travel is the glass of champagne on take-off, and shortly after eleven o'clock, few deserved it more than us. Or the abundant supply of Coca-Cola. The four of us had the section to ourselves, so we could drop the pretence of not knowing each other. But being overly cautious, I told Natasha not to speak whenever the stewardess came to serve food and drinks. She was my daughter and would remain so until we were safely on English soil. Airlines face heavy fines for carrying illegal immigrants to British airports, so it was still possible, if her identity became known, that Croatia Airlines might take her back to Zagreb rather than pay the penalty.

There was no reason why the charade should not have worked that entire flight without worry, but halfway through, the pilot came back to ask me if my daughter would care to sit with him in the cockpit, and before I could think of a reason to refuse politely, she was up there with him.

After what seemed ages, they came back busily chatting together. 'She is a charming little girl,' the captain said, 'and her Croat is almost word-perfect . . . I compliment you.' Unable to resist the cue, I replied, 'It's not really surprising . . . she's spent so much of her life abroad and she picks up languages so quickly, I think she'd learn Chinese just as well. It's time I kept her prisoner for a while so she can begin to speak proper English.' All five of us laughed, though only the four of us really knew why.

At Heathrow we went through the entry door marked 'Community Nationals Only', a sign which has always irked me. But at that moment I was not in that kind of mood and with teddy bear and T-shirt and the 'HI EVERYBODY!' bag, Natasha and I went happily towards the British Immigration officer's desk, walking, as the song goes, on air.

We shuffled forward in the short queue until it was my turn to hand him that precious little blue book with the gold-embossed crest. As he opened it, I turned, pointed to my companion and said, 'I think you should know that I have a little problem.'

CHAPTER FIVE

Like Alice, Natasha was finding her surroundings curiouser and curiouser. She was not at all sure what was and what was not, and like that other little girl who plunged into a rabbit-hole and discovered a crazy new world, she found herself dazed and dazzled by the bewildering assortment of sights, sounds and foreign bodies in Heathrow's Terminal Two. She had arrived on a wonderful summer's day to British Airport Authority glitz; wall-to-wall carpeting (even on the walls), and welcoming, smiling Asian ladies in chic blue uniforms pointing to Immigration queues that had no obvious beginning and no foreseeable end. Anxious to please, and with so much waiting time to spare, Natasha pushed baggage trolleys for jet-lagged Americans, deposited stray Coke cans into waste-bins and heaved a tiresome African two-year-old across the floor back to its mother who was less than pleased to see it, making Natasha wait, tottering under the weight of the fat little thing, until she had finished winding yards of purple silk around her enormous buttocks. It was thankfully Natasha's last act of charity, because thirty minutes after being told to wait for five, we were ushered into a British Immigration interview room by a polite man with a Cheshire-cat smile. We sat there patiently alongside a large Pakistani woman who was trying to soothe her crying child by bouncing it on her lap in the style of Alice's Duchess:

> Speak roughly to your little boy
> And beat him when he sneezes;
> He only does it to annoy,
> Because he knows it teases.

I too was experiencing the moment's unreality. It was not uncommon. Every time I returned to England from some crisis overseas, I felt the same sensation, as if all that had been real yesterday was suddenly phantom and imagined. I would pick up my bag from the carousel, push the baggage trolley through Customs and take a car home to a proper cuppa and cut grass and walk dogs and lose touch with time. The bloody carnage of yesterday's story had been distanced by the Jumbo jet and yesterday's pictures of sacrifice and suffering smothered by scented face towels at 35,000 feet; the memory denied, the therapy complete.

I had expected British Immigration officers to be hostile, cussed and uncooperative, and I was wrong three times over. To begin with, we had tea. Then a man who spoke Serbo-Croat sat with Natasha and told her, translating for me, that even though she was on holiday, she had to have a proper piece of paper to say she could stay in England. She agreed with him, not that anything he said really interested her. There were now so many other things to investigate. The Pakistani Duchess was noisily breast-feeding her child and the interview room was filling with people of more shapes, colours and tongues than Natasha could ever have imagined the world contained. Much encouraged, thanking the kind Serbo-Croat-speaking official and with the tea cups cleared away, she went from one bewildered foreign person to another, introducing herself and her story, bemusing and confusing, making them uncertain whether to bow or scrape or simply ignore.

I watched her and wondered. I remembered a coy, shy little girl in the orphanage in Sarajevo, who spoke only when she was spoken to and did what she was told as soon as she was told to do it. Now I was seeing something quite different and new developing, something blossoming, someone feeling the warm touch of the sun after a long time in the shadows. And as I watched, I had the first beginnings of doubt, an uncertainty about what it was I was importing and who it was I was now asking my family to accept as their own. Who was I now inviting into the nest? I felt like a cuckoo with a conscience.

With only Mrs Zoric's letter of authority as evidence, I told my story to three Immigration officers in turn, the last, a pleasant young lady, promising that once it had all been digested by the Home Office computer, I would be allowed to take Natasha home on a temporary visitor's permit. Within the hour we had it, authorization IS 96. giving her access with one restriction only . . . that she did not 'enter employment, paid or unpaid, or engage in any business or profession'. We agreed that all seemed reasonable enough. As we left, the young lady said, 'All of this has been rather fascinating . . . my father will be delighted when I tell him.' I asked why her father especially? 'He is in your business,' she replied. 'He's Mark Tully, the BBC's correspondent in India and a bit of an authority on refugees.'

Which was what Natasha had suddenly now become; a name, a number and a statistic on a Whitehall floppy disc. But orphan, refugee, what did it matter? We were home. Together we had made it. I rang Diana. 'We're through. They've let her in. We'll be with you in an hour.'

There was a moment's silence at the other end. Then simply, 'I'll be here. Well done!'

Then, with teddy bear, Mickey Mouse, carrier bag and all, the two of us walked out through the green channel – I had already declared the only thing that mattered – and out into Terminal Two Arrivals Hall to begin the last lap of our journey.

On the bookstand I saw the morning newspaper headline:

'BOSNIAN CRISIS. AMERICA CONSIDERS AIR STRIKES AGAINST SERBIA'.

It was a sham, of course, a bit of stick-waving and bravado in the run-up to the American Presidential elections. As in all campaigns at home and abroad, a lot of rubbish was spoken and a lot of pledges made. But the story that President George Bush was seeking wider powers from the UN to allow him to bomb targets in Serbia, even to send US ground troops to protect UN aid convoys, was nonsense. Neither he nor the voters were in the mood for it, nor, it was generally presumed then, would they ever be. Bosnia was a long, long way from Washington and as no American interests were threatened and American cars did not run on Balkan oil, the Americans concluded in their best tradition of self-interest and parochialism, that it was a European concern to be settled by the Europeans. Despite the daily reports of atrocities and vile human rights abuses, despite the carnage and suffering Mr and Mrs America saw nightly on their television news screens, they were not going to risk sending their sons and daughters to end it. The tragedy was that without America's military clout, the Europeans could do nothing except huff and puff, wring their hands and call the Serbs naughty names.

The immediate problem, given that the Serbs would not end their war, was to get food and medicines to the many besieged Muslim enclaves scattered across Bosnia which were under regular, almost daily, bombardment by the Serbs in their new-found strategy of shell-and-starve. A network of safe corridors allowing supplies to be distributed from the Croatian port of Split was proposed but according to defence experts the policing of such a *cordon sanitaire* would need over 100,000 troops. The arithmetic made the politicians shudder. They feared it would only aggravate the Serbs further, prolong the fighting and establish another Vietnam in the heart of Europe. They said what they were expected to say: that peace could only be achieved by negotiation.

The negotiators were less sure. Their principal, Lord Carrington, tired of shuttling between Belgrade and Zagreb and New York and Geneva, weary of lies, cunning, broken promises and endless ceasefire violations, had finally thrown in the towel and returned to selling antiques for Christie's. The diminutive, bespectacled aristocrat had been outpaced, out-gunned and outwitted by men he would not have employed to dig his gardens. He was the upright, courteous gentleman of the old school that somehow still believed that shaking hands sealed a contract and signatures a treaty. His five months of wrangling in chancellories, presidencies and embassies had achieved nothing. His diplomacy was dilettante, his grasp of the Balkan conundrum at best tenuous, his history was vague, he was unable to grasp the intricate geography, the unpronounceable names, the complicated tribalism. Fourteen years before, he had been hailed as the master mediator who forged Zimbabwe out of a civil war Rhodesia, ending seventeen years of UDI and giving the African power in his own land. It was thought he could do the same in former Yugoslavia, but he could not.

What was at stake now was not only to contain the war in Bosnia but to prevent it from exploding into a wider one across the Balkans and one that would pull in other nations as well. New alliances were showing themselves, and the Serbs, the new pariahs of Europe, were turning to old friends and allies in blood and faith, the principal exponents of the Slav and the Orthodox communities, Russia and Greece. Moscow had made it clear it would resist any persistent UN pressure on the Serbs and there were already rumours that the Russian military was helping with weapons and weapon-training. The most obvious flashpoint was Kosovo, the southern Serbian province which had an ethnic Albanian majority. It is the heart of medieval Serbia and the site of the Serbs' defeat by the Ottoman Turks in 1389, perhaps the most emotion-charged event in Serbian history. The Americans had privately warned the Serb leaders that Kosovo was the 'line in the sand' beyond which they must not tread. A war there would almost certainly ignite a full-scale Balkan conflict that would suck in Albania, Bulgaria and, worse, two NATO countries, Turkey and Greece, opposing each other. But that was such a frightening scenario, so the theory went, as to make it most improbable. That, too, was the prayer.

'It was brilliant . . . I could not believe it . . . I just could not believe it.'

Only now, so much later, can Natasha tell in her own English, something of what she remembers of that first day and her journey home to the wilds of outer Surrey. Sometimes we still wonder what images remain powerful and indelible in her mind and ask her to think back, but she will simply repeat, 'I could not believe it.' She knows she has yet to learn the English words that will adequately describe what she saw and how that July afternoon marked the baptism of her new life. She was Dorothy on the Yellow Brick Road; a crammed and hectic motorway; the roar of an airliner overhead, its wheels barely scraping the tree-tops; the bustle of High Street shopping; the climb up to the North Downs and over the Hog's Back to see below us the great sweep of woodlands south to the coast; and then the sudden shade of country lanes, the spangled light in avenues of oak and beech leading to the town where three counties meet and which she would very soon be calling her own. For over an hour she had sat and marvelled without speaking a word. At last she was in England and it was all she had imagined it to be, all she had dreamed everywhere to be like away from Sarajevo.

Finally, we came down the steep and winding hill into Brook village, past its immaculate green, until we came to our own village where, with the church clock about to chime four, we turned off the road into my garden and the waiting reception on the front steps; Diana, Tom, my eldest son, and the dogs, Max and Zimba. Diana was delightfully shy, which only emphasized how little I had thought of her and how she would react. She was, after all, the one who would have to cope full-time, at an age when many women were already assuming the role of grandmother or at least getting used to the prospect. Now, within a matter of days, she had prepared herself to be the surrogate mother to the little stranger who now stood hesitantly in front of her, a thin, pale Bosnian orphan, who spoke not a word of English, who had been plucked from a city at war and knew nothing of family life or the complicated ties that bind it together. The introductions made, they went indoors together, hand in hand, to tea and cakes and ice cream . . . and Natasha in no doubt she had made the right choice!

I spent much of that first day home making comparisons. I have already written that the very first thing I do on coming home from some foreign catastrophe is quickly to close the curtain on it. But now, as Natasha roamed nervous and curious from room to room, from cupboard to cupboard, I made an effort to resurrect the past week's images, transposing pictures of her in Sarajevo as she went about her new home in Surrey. She was introduced to my youngest son's William's bedroom, which would be hers until he returned from a four-month overland trip he was making to Katmandu. It was a cosy, warm and colourful room that took in all the day's sun, crowded with shelves of picture-books and broken crayons and dried-up paintboxes and wicker boxes overflowing with the mess of playthings long derelict. Natasha touched them, overwhelmed and amazed that so much should belong in one place to one person. Then I saw her in the dormitory of Ljubica Ivezic, with its ceiling streaked with fungus and the smell of urine and carbolic, not a single picture on the brown walls and not a single toy on any of the bunks.

Natasha followed Diana on a tour of the garden, soft lawns bordered by rhododendrons and a wisteria tree in the season's second blossom, under the massive cedar and the copper beech busy with squirrels and over a carpet of columbine through the line of dark oaks stretching down to the stream in the wood, watched beyond the orchard of apples and pears and plums by Tom and Hettie, our two donkeys. All these she inspected, saying nothing. And I thought back to the tiny face pressed against the criss-crossed sticky-taped window of broken glass after that first day's filming at the orphanage. The crew and I had crossed the mangle of cratered tarmac that had once been a playground, past the halfwit with the blood-streaked face, punishing and twisting the frightened, guilty kitten inside his pullover, pushing our way through the gang of older boys and girls, orphans all, noisy, filthy and ragged, who demanded vodka and cigarettes and tried to trip us and make us fall so they could steal the camera, having already stripped our Landrover of all its removables, even the stickers saying 'British Television'. Everything was worth something in Sarajevo then; where there is nothing, even rubbish has its worth. The girls were as tough and as determined as the boys, mixed helpings of wretchedness and wickedness, spending more of their days out of the orphanage than in it, patrolling the narrow streets and alleyways stealing, bullying. And I heard Mrs Zoric again; 'The boys will spend their lives in and out of prison and the girls will sell themselves.'

Natasha picked apples from the orchard and fed the donkeys and called them by their names, and everything was gold-tinted in the evening light as we all went indoors for dinner.

That night she cried herself to sleep. Such big tears, too, soaking the pillow. Happiness, sadness, tiredness, confusion, fright, as always made so much worse by the dark. And also the strange novelty of being in a bed of her own with no one to whisper to, no one to touch for comfort and only the occasional distant rumble of a late train interrupting a silence she had never known before. For the first time in her life she was alone. So Diana gathered her up and took her to our bed and I spent the remaining cramped and sleepless hours in one designed for someone a great deal smaller. I was there the next night too and the one after that, and I feared it might well become a regular thing.

Diana and I had agreed from the start that we would keep our new lodger's real identity secret. As far as outsiders were concerned, she was the daughter of a friend in Bosnia and was staying with us until the end of the summer holiday. That was true to Mrs Zoric's letter at least. There would be no talk of fostering or adoption and certainly nothing about how I had smuggled her to Britain. Publicity was bound to harm Natasha and any plans we had for her future with us. It was not such a pretence. Diana felt more at ease and better able to cope if she and I could agree that Natasha was only with us on a wait-and-see basis. It seemed a very sensible precaution; after all, we had no legal jurisdiction over her, and both the British and Bosnian governments could demand her return in the unlikely event of a quick Balkan peace. It was also possible that Natasha might eventually make her own decision that she did not want to stay with us, even if she wished to remain in England. But the bottom line was that, given our age, given that we had already brought up one family of boys, given the anxiety about Natasha's background, given the worry about schools, O levels, A levels and so on and so on, we might simply conclude we could not begin it all over again. Natasha was on holiday and that is what we told her and all those who got to know her.

Until that early-morning knock on my front door and the young lady who introduced herself as Kim Bartlett, a reporter from the *Sun* newspaper. After small-talk about the pretty garden and the view and apologies for arriving unannounced, she said, 'We gather you have brought a war baby back from Bosnia.'

To be a passable television reporter it is necessary to be something of an actor too, and at that moment I was thankful for the training. I laughed, perhaps a little too good-naturedly, considering the hour, tied the belt of my dressing-gown tighter, denied everything very convincingly and asked how she had managed to concoct such an idiotic story.

'British Immigration at Heathrow told us.' A lesser man might have been beaten by that, but a lot was at stake. As bare-faced lies are the best form of defence, and remembering Samuel Butler's advice that the best liar makes the smallest amount of lying go a long way, I said that on my way out of Bosnia I had indeed been asked to take children with me and had been very tempted to help. But how could I? Both my sons had left home and I spent more of my time away from England than in it.

Who would I bring a baby home to? Somebody was talking mischievous nonsense and if she could find out who it was I would advise my solicitors.

She went off down the drive, walking slowly, hesitating. Had it worked? Was she convinced? She was not! An hour later she was back with a photographer, and this time there was no talk about garden views and no apologies. She had checked again with the Home Office. They had confirmed that I had been seen with a little girl at Terminal Two on an inbound flight from Zagreb, and contrary to the rules – there was a brand-new press officer on duty that day – they had even confirmed my name.

It was game, set and match, and time for the barricades. Very soon we were under siege, with *Sun* reporters and photographers at every strategic point in our garden. The deployment began at around ten o'clock and by mid-afternoon they had been reinforced. I peered out from behind curtains, prisoner in my own house. I knew the signs. They were preparing for a long stake-out and any moment a mobile kitchen was bound to appear with flasks of tea and coffee and buckets of Kentucky Fried. Every other minute they called me on their Cellnets, pleading, demanding, threatening, accusing, conspiring. I disconnected the telephone, double-locked the doors and pondered my next move. I knew they could certainly outwait me, they had the time, the determination and encouragement from a ruthless news editor. It was time for damage-limitation. Dog was about to eat dog. I knew the rules. Tell a newspaper reporter nothing and he will invent a story. Aggravate and obstruct him and he will do you harm. I would have to tell the *Sun* my story, I had no choice now. But later rather than sooner. Natasha needed more time to settle, to remain anonymous and be protected a little longer from the inevitable battery of cameras and barrage of questions and the publicity that would follow. It was a dilemma I had not expected to face so quickly and I was not certain how to handle it. But my editor-in-chief could and did. He quickly arranged that the *Sun* would end their siege, on my undertaking to give them an exclusive story when, and only when, I was ready to, perhaps in a week or two. So it was agreed, and the besiegers went away. My house and garden became mine again and Diana and Natasha came out of hiding.

Then came the second unexpected invasion: the Social Welfare Officer. The Home Office, as a matter of routine, had alerted Surrey County Council, who in turn advised Waverley Borough Council who then told the Haslemere Social Services Centre, who promptly sent a Family Placement Social Worker to inspect and report on our suitability as surrogate parents. It was all rather unexpected and a bit of a shock. Less than a week before, Natasha had been an orphan, a war waif; then, on arrival in England, she had become a refugee seeking asylum. Now, in the jargon of the Children's Act 1989 (Private Arrangements for Fostering Regulations-Amendments 1991), she was a 'child in foster-care'.

Events were beginning to overwhelm me. Big Brother, or rather Big Sister, had taken us in hand. I was given circular SS136 (Revised), four closely typed pages listing the Social Welfare Department's powers over Natasha's future. It was numbing. It threatened a Case Manager (Children and Families), who would shortly come and inspect us and 'the whole or any part of the premises' and return for the same purpose every six weeks. She would also want to interview Natasha alone, which sounded both sinister and unsupportive. We were also told that we did not have responsibility for her simply by assuming it and that it might well be the eventual opinion of the Authority that she would be better 'placed' with a family of the same ethnic background. I was told that the child's needs 'arising from religious persuasion, racial, cultural and linguistic origins' were paramount, when I, naïve soul, had simply wanted to save her from howitzer shells and 120-mm mortars. Finally, every member of my family was obliged to sign a form consenting to a police check on their criminal records; failure to cooperate or to 'wilfully make or cause to be made false statements' would render us liable to imprisonment.

My first reaction, of course, was to rant and rage, but I could not be too angry publicly. The Social Welfarers have their own no-win Catch 22; if they do their job properly, they need to be inquisitive and intrusive and almost clinically thorough. And when they do not, they get flak. But there was another reason to cooperate. Should we one day want to adopt Natasha, a testimony from our Case Manager supporting us would be vital to our application: the requirements in the Act concerning 'standard of care' and 'suitability of the foster-parents' needed her approval.

Early on, our suitability had a few narrow squeaks. Natasha was teaching herself to ride a bicycle and, in character, stubbornly refused help. Doggedly she tried again and again, each time freewheeling a little longer than the last but always ending in a wet and muddy mangled pile of spinning wheels and twisted handlebars. Finally, on the third day and with great whoops of joy, she triumphantly outwitted gravity and accomplished one of the great milestones in a child's growing-up: she could ride. But at what a price! Her arms and legs were a patchwork of bruises, grazes and tattered elastoplasts and until she had recovered, Diana and I waited apprehensively for the Case Manager's visit. Her obvious and wrong conclusion would not have read well in court.

'She wants to know how long she will stay so she knows how much love she must give.' That sentence and all it represented for Natasha and for us was ever constant in our minds. We had told her that she was just on holiday, so it was not surprising that she should keep her emotions in check until she was more sure of her future. She would have to govern the pace of the affection she gave and expected to receive, and she was content to enjoy each day as it happened, not looking back, not looking too far forward. Maybe that is every child's way.

We spent much of that first week exploring the labyrinth of footpaths and bridleways in the hills and woods overlooking our village. As Natasha's English was still non-existent and my

Serbo-Croat restricted to 'Dobadan' (Good day), 'Molimo' (Please), 'Dobra', (Good) and 'Hvala' (Thank you), conversation was limited. But they were lovely, warm, cloudless summer days in one of the prettiest parts of our county and they were important in helping Natasha adapt to the sudden and complete change in her life.

The regimented existence in the orphanage (for the younger children at least) had taught her discipline, and to begin with nothing was out of order. She made her bed in the morning, hung up her clothes neatly, polished her shoes and, to our surprise and a little embarrassment, was happy to wash the dishes and mop the kitchen floor. She was unlike any English girl of her age in her habits. But little by little as the days moved into weeks and the weeks into months, all this was to change as she copied the ways of her new English friends, staying with them overnight and sometimes at weekends and seeing how pleasantly different the new discipline was from Mrs Zoric's. Like any little girl, she adapted to it quickly.

Diary entry, Monday, 3 August: 'The honeymoon is over. Anonymous and unsuspecting Natasha is about to become famous and in public demand world-wide. Heaven help us!'

The *Sun* editor had at last demanded his pound of flesh. I had given my interview, they had taken their photographs, and we had awaited their publication. You might imagine that having been in the trade for over thirty years, I could have predicted what followed. I expected a small story and a small photo tucked away somewhere between the gossip and sport pages or any dignified distance from the alarming Page Three. I did not expect a front-page headline and a double centre-page spread in colour with a photograph of me in Royal Navy helmet and flak-jacket (taken ten years before in the Falklands) beneath the headline 'I RISKED ARREST TO SAVE ORPHAN FROM WAR'. My story was wedged between 'MERCURY CUTS OFF LINES IN SEX CLEAN-UP' and 'BOSS PROBED OVER SEX

ACT AT DESK', but it was told accurately despite the traditional tabloid hyperbole. What had had to be done was now done and Diana and I reckoned we had got off lightly. Natasha had been introduced to the *Sun* readership and we could again get on with the task of absorbing our little Bosnian visitor into our lives quietly and uninterrupted.

Not so! Not by a long chalk. By ten-thirty that Monday morning there were over thirty reporters and photographers on our front lawn and within the hour they had been joined by a dozen more. By midday, the ITN outside broadcast unit was parked by the fish-pond. The Fourth Estate had taken over. Natasha had become public property.

The *Sun* story had done what I must subconsciously have known it would do, and the opposite of what I had hoped. It generated an explosion of interest bordering on the manic. I could appreciate that a tabloid scoop might cause some fury on its opposition's news desks, enough perhaps for them to attempt a follow-up, looking for a different angle to the story. But that did not explain why every national newspaper, with the exception of the *Financial Times* and the *Guardian*, had arrived, including reporters from the major Continental dailies and from Scandinavia, Chile, Brazil and Canada. I was inundated with transatlantic telephone requests for live satellite interviews with the American networks ABC and CNN and there was even an invitation to fly, all expenses paid, to appear on a television forum in Tokyo. I told my story forty times over that morning in response to the vaguely hostile, cross-examining way reporters have of interviewing. Was it right or was it wrong to do what I did? Was I headstrong, emotionally unstable, professionally at odds? Ethics, politics, morality, they tried their best to find a new line, but finally they settled for a good old-fashioned human interest yarn . . . a war story with a happy ending, the only good news to come out of Sarajevo.

Then it was time for Natasha and me to pose for the photographers. We posed together, apart, we posed playing cricket, playing football, netball, tennis; we posed sitting with the cats, sitting with the dogs, standing by the cows, by the donkeys, by the wisteria; we fed the doves, the cats, the dogs, the donkeys, each other! Our faces ached with smiles and our friendship began to feel the strain. Then it was over and they all went away and I concluded that, given a nice story, my fellow hitmen and hitwomen are really quite nice too. But there was an exception that day which caused some grief.

'Bare your soul and they will publish the warts and all.' It is excellent cautionary advice when dealing with the media and I should know. I had nothing to hide and there was nothing that could not be told, yet as many know to their cost (and some lucky ones to their libelled financial advantage), reporters can, for all kinds of motives, cause mischief where none is deserved.

> You cannot hope to bribe or twist
> Thank God, the British journalist
> For seeing the man will unbribed do
> There's no occasion to.

Rebecca Hardy of the *Daily Mail* had been very persistent throughout, probably vexed that the *Sun*'s Kim Bartlett had scooped her. Well known for her dogged enthusiasm, she pursued me around the garden asking me again and again why Diana had not made an appearance, why she had not given interviews and posed with Natasha. What had happened to the rest of my family? asked the insistent Miss Hardy. I explained that Diana was extremely shy of the press – a shyness that has bordered at times on dangerous hostility – so that when she saw the posse of newsmen come in through the front gate she rapidly exited unseen through the back. There was, I explained, nothing sinister or devious about it; that had always been her way, to distance her life and her family from my own public profile, refusing interviews and all the associated rubbish about life with a war correspondent, the women who wait, etc., etc. But Miss Hardy would not be put off and I guessed why. I knew her angle . . . a preconception cloaked in controversy and never-let-the-facts-get-in-the-way-of-a-good story! And sure enough the next day the *Daily Mail* led with her front-page story implying that Natasha had caused a rift between Diana and me. It was headlined 'WIFE'S ANXIETIES FOR SARAJEVO REFUGEE'.

> Wife Diana was not consulted before her husband decided
> to flee with Natasha and now complains that the
> responsibility of bringing up the young girl will fall largely
> on her shoulders . . . and is adamant that her husband
> must eventually take her back. Diana insists the little girl
> does not call her Mummy.

Jill Parkin, a columnist on the *Daily Express*, was quick on the chase with 'ACT OF MERCY THAT CAN ONLY LEAVE THE WIFE SHELLSHOCKED'.

> No matter how much she enjoyed having children . . . Diana
> must have been looking forward to some life of her own.
> Now it will start again . . . at school gates at the age of fifty.
> And her husband will be off to the wars again, coming
> home to do all the fun things absent daddies do. No wonder
> Diana is insisting the little girl does not call her mummy.
> She will be the one on duty every day. Michael's impulse
> may have been humanitarian. But was it good husbandry?

Others in my own media, though strangers, conducted their own public condemnation of me. There were reports that I would be prosecuted for forging my passport, even that I should be, because I had abused my privileged position as a known television correspondent. I listened, though I was never invited to participate, to radio interviews in which Those-Who-Know-Everything condemned me for taking only one child out and consequently causing misery for those left behind; of causing unfathomable damage to Natasha's psyche by removing her from her natural environment and plunging her into alien country. I wondered if those fools knew of anything more damaging than the mortars falling on Sarajevo or how completely destructive a howitzer shell is to the environment there. And what effect did they consider an explosive bullet, guided by the sniper's ever-watchful telescopic sight, had upon the psyche of men, women and children who needed to cross open ground to get to the fresh-water tap or go without drink for another day? They should have asked the orphans I found huddled in dank cellars without fresh air or daylight, which environment they preferred. Instead of ranting on Radio Three, they should have asked Natasha where she chose to be: Sarajevo or Surrey?

I was accused of violating a sacrosanct rule of journalism (though I have to admit it was new to me), viz: Never Get Involved. I read that I had 'ignited fervent debate in the newsrooms of Europe', which seemed most improbable. Some journalists were apparently 'appalled that Nicholson sacrificed for ever his ability to report impartially'. All of which was codswallop. From the beginning, ITN had been nonplussed by the event, hesitant and uncertain how to play it. My editor-in-chief had not been prepared to break the story, but had decided (wisely, I think in retrospect), to leave it to the newspapers. ITN could then be seen to follow up ever so reluctantly and, for good form, a trifle hostile. Nick Owen, the lunchtime news presenter, began his live interview with me thus:

Q: There is an unwritten rule, isn't there, that journalists shouldn't get involved?

A: Nick, I don't know who wrote that rule, I haven't met the man who did. It certainly hasn't hindered me, nor any journalist I have ever respected, dead or alive. I know there are those who insist we should stay on the sidelines, but the problem with that is you tend to see things from a distance and a reporter's first duty is to get as close to the story as possible. Of course, if you get too close you run the risk of ending up a casualty. You could say I'm a casualty of Sarajevo, but, as you see, quite a willing one.

At the end of that day it was difficult to believe that Natasha had ever been a casualty of war, she had coped so easily, so naturally, thoroughly enjoying herself, doing as she was told to do and delighted to be doing it. Perhaps she considered it a payment in kind, and a little one too, all things considered.

CHAPTER SIX

The razzmatazz of going public was over. For a few days Natasha had enjoyed celebrity status and been paid the attention normally reserved for starlets and tennis prodigies. It had been fun. But the very next morning I was shocked back to reality, and the timing could not have been more cruel. If there were those who still had doubts about the horrors Natasha had escaped or the risks she had shared in the escaping, that morning's news must surely have dispelled them. Two little children, babies still, had been shot dead by snipers as a second convoy had tried to leave Sarajevo. Fourteen-month-old Roki Sulejmanovic, a Muslim boy, and two-year-old Vedrana Glavas, a Serb girl, had been killed when four bullets hit their coach.

Encouraged by the success of our first evacuation, the First Children's Embassy in Sarajevo had attempted another, with fifty more children aged between eight weeks and four years, from the Ljubica Ivezic orphanage. Natasha would have known them all. But the organizers had rushed it. Anxious to get the children out, they had ignored all the known dangers of that perilous exit. They had even put the children aboard the two coaches outside the charity's headquarters near to the city centre, which, as everyone had warned, was one of the most dangerous areas, in full view of the snipers and the artillery spotters on the hills. The killers could not have had a better, earlier warning. Worse still, the coaches left at seven in the evening, and everyone knew it was always at dusk that the separate armies prepared themselves for yet another assault on each other from the hillsides flanking Sniper's Alley, the road the coaches would have to travel.

When we had left a fortnight before, we had the agreement of a temporary ceasefire and a UN escort of armoured cars. But this second convoy and its precious cargo left that evening with neither safeguard, and as it turned on to the dual carriageway and the airport road, the lead coach swerved and slewed sideways. The first bullet shattered the windscreen, the second blew out the front tyre, the third and fourth killed Roki and Vedrana. For some moments, the coaches were stranded in no man's land. Some of the adults aboard screamed at the drivers to go back, others to go forward, pulling the children to the floor, covering them with handbags and suitcases, waiting for the next burst of gunfire. Then, despite his blown front tyre, the lead driver drove on and the second followed, twisting and bumping their way slowly through the streets of gutted houses in a wasteland of rubble, until they came to the first Croat road-block, safely beyond the killer's sights. There, they wrapped the two little bodies in blankets and gave them to the soldiers, asking that they should somehow get them back to Sarajevo. Then, having changed the front tyre, they drove on into the night to find a safe place until morning.

But the drama was not over. They took a wrong road and were stopped by Serb soldiers who boarded the coaches, searching, they said, for weapons and any Muslim fighters attempting to escape. After interrogation, they discovered that nine of the children were of Serb origin, so they carried them off screaming and kicking and they were not seen or heard of again.

When the bodies of Riko and Vedrana and the story of how they had died reached Sarajevo, recrimination threatened the entire evacuation project. Dusko Tomic, founder of the First Children's Embassy, defended his decision to send the convoy, saying that it had already been delayed a week because of renewed fighting in the suburbs. But most damning for him and his sponsors was his admission that despite all the known risks, the German charity that had arranged to meet the convoy and take it on to the coast where their aircraft was waiting to fly the children to foster homes in Germany, had urged him to hurry because further delays would cost them more. So Tomic had hurried to save the Germans their money, at the price of two little lives.

The tragedy was compounded a day later, and again the timing was grotesque coincidence. In Sarajevo there is no dignity in death. Even the final moment of remembrance is invariably denied the dead and those who come to mourn them, and so it was that morning when the families of the two little children arrived at the cemetery to bury them. Vedrana's mother had picked a small bunch of wild flowers and her grandmother Ruza had nailed two rough bits of wood into a cross. It was never safe to stand in the open for too long in that city, even in a cemetery, and the service, like all in that place then, was intended to be short and simple, the business of burial a brisk affair. But it had barely begun when the first mortar landed 100 yards away in the ice rink built for the 1984 Olympics. As the mourners scrambled for cover, four more shells landed among the gravestones, exploding into a thousand splinters of stone and metal. The mourners crawled to the cover of the trees but Ruza lay writhing and groaning by the open grave of her grandchild, her right arm almost severed at the shoulder. No one dared move into the open again to help her until they thought it was safe to do so and only then did they carry Ruza away with women following, weeping and shaking with shock.

Soon after they had gone, the gravediggers came out of the bunker they had dug for themselves and dropped the two tiny boxes into the hole, one on top of the other, and quickly heaped on the earth; two children snatched out of their cots and bundled away on a journey of escape that had ended so soon in a shallow grave, without grace or prayer or ceremony. And high up on the mountain slopes watching the gravediggers smooth the last spadeful, the killers lit another cigarette and smiled to each other, satisfied with their morning's work.

There was another casualty in Sarajevo that day but I was not to know about it until much later. On the evening of the burial, police went to the Ljubica Ivezic orphanage and interviewed its director, Vera Zoric. They told her that they held her responsible for the deaths of Roki and Vedrana because she had prime authority and she had given permission for them to be taken out of Sarajevo. They said that she was guilty of criminal negligence and could expect to be arrested, and they left with the warning that they would return once the charge had been formalized.

Vera Zoric was a sensible and brave woman who was quite prepared to defend herself in court. She would argue that it was her first duty to protect her children. Look, she would say, see the damage to my building, see how the children must stay in the cellars, count the babies who have never seen daylight or breathed fresh air, count the mortar bombs that have landed around us. How much closer must they come before I evacuate? How much longer must I wait until the authorities take my children to safety? I did what I thought was best, she would say, and if two of my babies were killed on their way to freedom then forty-eight others have escaped. She was certain the equation was her convincing defence.

But early the following morning, word came to her via a short, quick telephone call, that the police were on their way to arrest her. And the warrant was not for criminal negligence. It was for murder.

When the four policemen arrived at the orphanage, they found the director's office empty. Vera Zoric had gone. For the next month she managed to evade them, moving from one safe house to another, always a step ahead, until eventually she escaped Sarajevo and went to the only people she knew would look after her. It was such a bitter irony. Vera Zoric was a Bosnian Serb, so she had crossed the mountains to the town of Pale, the Bosnian-Serb headquarters. She had been forced to seek refuge among her own people, the very people who had caused her such distress, who had for six months been shelling her city and her orphanage. The people who had murdered two of her children.

Fifteen children were killed in Sarajevo the day Riko and

Vedrana were buried, and thirty-two adults as well. It was a high figure, forty-seven dead in one day, but it was not unusual. In the bread-queue massacre that May, when a mortar fell into a crowded shopping street, nineteen men and women had died instantly and twice as many were wounded, some maimed for life. Then, in eleven seconds, in what became known as the water-queue massacre later that summer, another thirteen were killed just as efficiently. Relentlessly, day in, day out, week on week, month after month, Bosnia's casualties rose so that by the end of 1992, nine months after the war began, upwards of 30,000 people had been killed, among them 8000 children. At the war's first anniversary in April 1993, the death toll had reached over 130,000, 16,000 of the victims children under the age of fourteen.

But the atrocities committed in war have many faces, and not all those who died in this one were casualties of the random mortar and incendiary bomb or even the sniper's casual bullet. Many died looking into their killer's eyes, victims of cold-blooded mass murder.

Just as the Serbs had reminded the world, by their ethnic cleansing, of Hitler's pogroms against the Jews, so they re-introduced to the world's consciousness, the concentration camp. These were euphemistically called 'detention centres', transit camps of a sort where thousands of Muslim men and women, the lucky survivors of ethnic cleansing, were herded together and interrogated and, if they were luckier still, eventually rescued by the UN or the Red Cross and moved to safer quarters.

Omarska and Trnopolje were two Serb detention camps visited and filmed by ITN reporters Penny Marshall and Ian Williams and their crews in August last year. Their reports were the first graphic examples of how brutal the Serbs were to those they captured. It also showed how inept the Serbs were in their efforts to improve their 'international image', because – astonishing as it now seems – the purpose of inviting the media into the camps was for precisely that reason. The Bosnian–Serb leader Dr Radavan Karadzic had given ITN permission to visit

Omarska and Trnopolje thinking they would illustrate how kindly Muslim prisoners of war were being treated, knocking the notion of Serb cruelty on the head once and for all. Karadzic was a fool and those who advised him bigger fools if they did not know of the conditions in those camps and the devastating effect their exposure would have. Never had there been such a public relations blunder. When the pictures of the camp's inmates were shown in that first week of August, the vivid images of men behind wire, the taut rib-cages, the sunken cheeks, the skeletal young man later named as Filcret Alich, the servile prisoners and their fearsome camp commandants, was all so evocative of Herr Himmler's Final Solution, it created a massive and immediate international response. Nothing better illustrated the ability of television to make the world's foreign policy makers jump.

The United States as well as Britain and most European countries had known about Serb atrocities for months. Newspapers had reported ethnic cleansing and all its associated horrors, supported by dates, places, eye-witness accounts, photographs. Conditions in the detention camps had also been meticulously documented. The UN High Commission for Refugees had distributed to 4700 diplomats and journalists a detailed report specifically about Omarska and Trnopolje. Few paid the slightest attention. Yet one short television report of apparently starving Muslims stripped to the waist behind a barbed-wire fence surrounded by grim, gun-toting Serb guards, was like an electric shock to the wise men who govern us. Overnight, politicians on both sides of the Atlantic trembled with outrage and were deafening in their denunciations. President Bush was told to miss his breakfast when his aides saw ITN's pictures on CNN and immediately called a press conference. Those who attended considered it well worth the effort; George Bush moved to passion was something that only happened in the closing months of a Presidential election year. The UN Security Council was called on to do whatever it deemed necessary to restore basic human rights in Bosnia and Britain's ambassador to the UN was told not to mince his words in supporting the motion. Members of Parliament went into a frenzy of televised outrage, forcing Prime Minister Major to announce, much against his own wishes, that Britain might be impelled to intervene with force (though only if the Americans elected for military action too). The wealthier countries of the European Community declared they would collectively find room for the thousands of detainees held in the camps and provide the sick with the necessary medical treatment and con-valescence. It really did seem, in that week in August, that the wheels were turning at last and that the patience of those men in high places who could do something to end Bosnia's dying and suffering had finally been exhausted.

Sadly, it had not. Prime Minister Major, who was then acting President of the European Community, hosted a peace conference in London and hastily declared it an enormous suc-cess after the warring factions separately signed an eleven-point peace plan. The Serbs, cocking a snook at their British host and everything they had put their names to in his presence, went back to their war and gave Sarajevo its worst ever bombard-ment, killing forty-seven people in twenty-four hours of relent-less shelling. Milan Panic, the American émigré maverick, sometime bankrupted millionaire-cum-Prime Minister of the Yugoslav rump, said he would order the Bosnian Serbs to close the detention camps forthwith. 'I give myself thirty days to do so,' he promised the world via Eurovision. More importantly, he also revealed that there were nearly 100 such camps, far more than anyone had guessed, and the figure was not denied by the Bosnian Serbs. But Mr Panic was a clown who simply did not have the political clout to do anything but play charades in front of the cameras.

In Washington, the White House and the State Department, always scary of the nightly network television news shows, began to relax their war rhetoric as news producers (universally contrary) quickly forgot the images of the camps and pushed Bosnia down the news agenda to make room for another report on the Presidential campaign trail.

Interest and indignation gave way to indifference. The change in pace created a logjam of human suffering. The Croats, who had taken in nearly one million refugees, had now closed their border to any more. Germany, denounced for provoking the war by prematurely accepting the break-up of the Yugoslav Republic, had agreed to accept half a million, perhaps as a penance. Austria said it was prepared to take 73,000, Sweden 80,000.

Britain was not so generous. The government was very particular about who it gave visas to. One junior minister at the Home Office remarked that Britain had no obligation to open its immigration doors to people who, in his words, 'merely want a better life', even though for the past fifty years Britain had left its immigration doors wide open to many millions of Asians and West Indians who simply wanted just that. The minister's remark summed up the British government's myopia on Bosnia. He seemed not to have noticed that the many thousands of Muslim Slavs who were now seeking refuge in Britain had never wanted to come here or anywhere else until the Serbs took their homes from them. Nor, come to that, would they have left at all, if the Serbs, having conquered them and established their territorial claim, had left Muslim homes and crops standing. But they did not. Their strategy of burn-and-bomb, shell-and-starve, left people with nothing, absolutely nothing, except the prospect of certain death if they stayed. So they fled across borders looking for sanctuary, not because they were greedily taking advantage of the chaos of war to seek a more comfortable life of social welfare benefits, but because few had any choice.

But the British government stubbornly maintained its stance, geographic if not entirely moral, insisting that Bosnian refugees should be confined within the borders of former Yugoslavia. To do otherwise, we were piously reminded, would be to assist, not deter, the Serbs in their ethnic cleansing. Eventually, after some fervent lobbying and a very hostile media, the British Home Secretary was forced to concede and he expanded the quota to 40,000 refugees, but only on a strictly enforced 'need-to-come' basis. It was a meagre gesture in the circumstances, when hundreds of thousands were in such desperate plight on the Croatian border and when, as it was generally believed, most would want to return to their country when the war was finally over.

The government did accept sixty-eight badly wounded Muslim prisoners of war from northern Bosnia but when, at the end of September, the UN asked the seventeen most prosperous European nations to keep the promise they had made only a few months earlier, to receive the Muslim prisoners of Omarska and Trnopolje, most, including Britain, failed to respond.

The Serbs interpreted this international apathy as bordering on neutrality and were much encouraged. Instead of closing the detention camps, they expanded them to hasten the evacuation of Muslims from land and towns the Serbs had earmarked for themselves. In short, they stepped up the rate of ethnic cleansing.

Word went around the threatened Muslim villages and farmlands that the UN and the International Red Cross were to empty the camps and not only transfer the inmates to safe, friendlier sites but somehow to magic them away to sympathetic foreign countries. Thousands of terrified Muslim families, knowing they were about to lose everything anyway, flocked to the camps. But the numbers overwhelmed the strategy and instead of the camps emptying, they became more crowded and the conditions in them even more squalid. According to one American Intelligence report there were more than 70,000 people in such camps.

The onset of the winter winds and rains compounded the suffering, and people who only weeks before had been harvesting land that had been theirs for generations, now sat under plastic sheets on wet blankets amid flooded makeshift lavatories disgorging sewage into rivers of mud. Those who had strength enough grovelled for cold rice in filthy kitchens, their children crushed lice in their hair and picked at their sores. Mothers gave birth by candlelight and kept their babies in cardboard boxes.

Some, in their desperation and despair, crawled to the camp's perimeter fence and threw their newborn over the wire to perish unseen, unheard. In September, I reported from Karlovac, from an old army barracks converted by the UNHCR as a reception centre, on the first release of prisoners from Trnopolje. My commentary to ITN that evening began:

> All had their stories to tell, personal testimonies to their captors' cruelty. They speak of rape, torture, death by beating. This mother, seven months pregnant, said women (some were only young girls) were giving birth in the camps and taking babies to the woods to die. Some strangled them, some buried them alive. Some just left them to die in the dark.
>
> The men had something new and more sinister to tell. They said that the educated prisoners, the doctors, teachers, the political and religious leaders among them, had been segregated and killed. Hasan Delic was one of many witnesses. The guards, he said, came and read out the names. We knew they were educated men, or wealthy, he said. They were taken out of our barracks and beaten . . . we could hear them screaming. I saw the bodies the next morning in the yard. The strongest among us had to carry them away to lorries. Men were covered in blood for days, until it rained and they could wash it off.

I ended my report: 'Today a new word has entered the vocabulary of this war. It is Eliticide.'

The camps must close! Our indignant politicians had insisted they must and they had given their word on it. But the camps remained open and conditions in them were now far, far worse than anything the earlier ITN pictures had shown. And the suffering was shared now not only by the men but by their women and children too. And still nothing was done.

On 25 September, something new was reported and, if those reports were to be believed, something infinitely more wicked.

The BBC's monitoring station at Caversham in Berkshire had picked up a broadcast by Radio Bosnia alleging that special concentration camps existed for women only. It also said that the Serbs were holding more than 10,000 prisoners in them for the purpose of systematic rape. Many of the camps were located close to military barracks and some were former hotels or restaurants; one was named; the Sonja Motel, a few miles on the Serb side of Sarajevo. Entire villages, it was alleged, had been converted to 'rape camps' and Miljevina in eastern Bosnia was named as one of many. The broadcasts which followed and were monitored by Caversham, became more explicit. Women were being raped in public for general entertainment; the favourites who cooperated were given protected status and special favours; those who resisted had their throats cut; those who failed to please were sent on to other, harsher regimes.

The story erupted. The media rushed headlong to find victims and very soon were even competing for them. A Croatian feminist group in Zagreb, sponsored by similar activists in Germany, sent out an open letter to other women's organizations in Europe and North America, listing 'survivors' testimonies' as well as the location of sixteen rape camps. In one, the letter alleged, 'girls of ten and even younger are raped and twelve women who managed to escape are now in advanced stages of pregnancy in a Zagreb hospital.' The letter, which naturally received world-wide publicity, ended with the most damning conclusion, albeit without any evidence to support it, that the rapes were not casual, bestial acts by undisciplined or drunken soldiers, 'but a tactic and strategy of genocide'.

The story created its own momentum with the reported scale of the crimes rising daily. In Germany and France, prominent articles appeared in *Stern, Der Spiegel* and *Libération*, along with warning preambles that some of the victims' testimonies were so horrific that they could not be printed, which may or may not have been an invidious circulation ploy. What was printed was hardly less than horrific. Accounts told of assaults on children as young as six, the rape of neighbour by neighbour, of multiple gang rapes so brutal that the victims died, of women whose ovaries were so dislodged that they could not walk, of daughters raped in front of fathers, mothers, siblings, of how those who survived their ordeal were ordered to wash the floors and swab down the walls of the blood of those who had not.

There was much confusion, contradiction and downright biological impossibility in many of the accounts. But what was in no doubt was that people not only wanted to read them but believe them. Newspapers and magazines carried full-page petitions demanding collective international action, including one that urged that the Foreign Legion be parachuted into 'known' rape camps to kill the captors and free the captives. But it was the accusation, originating from Bonn and Zagreb and now widely canvassed, that rape was a Serb strategy of genocide that most fired the imagination.

The Serb High Command, it was alleged, was using rape as a weapon of war. Believing, as the Serbs so earnestly do (and as the Nazis once did), that nationality is based on descent, it follows that the greatest debasement is to pollute a person's descendants. So, having systematically conquered and emptied so much of Muslim Bosnia, having either killed the menfolk or banished them to concentration camps, the mass rape of their closeted women and their impregnation with Serb blood, was the ultimate *coup de grâce*. Bosnian religious, cultural and national identity was destroyed for ever by a single sexual act. That was one theory. There was another, and again it smacked of Nazi Germany: that the Serbs were modelling their camps on the baby farms and the joy camps set up by Himmler, where women were kept to be enjoyed by weary war heroes in need of rest, recuperation and abundant sex. In this way the Serbs were assured that by seeding Muslim women, a whole new Serb bloodline was being established, a generation that would one day fill the empty parts of a country that once had the impertinence to call itself Bosnia but had long since become part of Greater Serbia.

But the most staggering of all the allegations was the number of victims said to be involved. An EC mission led by a woman and consisting only of women, came to the conclusion, after a surprisingly brief investigation and without even daring to visit Bosnia itself, that upwards of 10,000 Muslim women and girl children had been raped. Feminist organizations who had hoped to use the mission's report were disappointed at such a low estimate and preferred instead to stick with the figure used by the Bosnian government which ranged from 30,000 to 50,000 depending on which government department was asked. If true, this amounted to the greatest human rights violation against women of any war this half-century, perhaps even of this century. But an indictment of such enormity demanded more, much more than the scant evidence that was provided. Where, it was asked, did the figures come from? Who in such a short time and with all the dangerous impracticalities of travelling around a war zone, had managed to compile the list, given that so many of the women involved must still be prisoners of the Serbs? Who was orchestrating the numbers game and why? As somebody wrote at the time, it all depended on who was doing the counting. If you were Bosnian you thought of a number and simply added the noughts. If you were a Serb you cancelled it out completely.

Since the initial allegations a year ago, the Bosnian government has admitted that its figures were guestimates and extrapolations based on a very small number of interviews and third-person testimonies. There were some confessions by captured Serbs, like the twenty-one-year-old Borislav Herak, who admitted raping seven Muslim women and killing twenty, for which he was sentenced to hang by a court in Sarajevo this year. There were also the two young Serb deserters Slobodan Panic and Cvijetin Maksimovic who confessed they were ordered to rape for their commander's amusement. But then, as somebody observed at the time, they would say that, wouldn't they?

What remains is the evidence, not of thousands of women, but of no more than a hundred, and too much of that is anecdotal, too much of it hearsay and at third person removed. To date, the International Red Cross has received no first-hand testimonies to confirm the existence of the so-called rape camps, and none of the known human rights agencies, including the UN High Commission for Refugees, can corroborate the claims. Both those institutions, with singularly uncharacteristic candour, have warned that the numbers should be treated with caution. Finally, and given even the mean estimate of 10,000 rapes, where are the women now? Where are their babies? Surely, in those months when the story was rife with accusations and investigations (ITN sent its own woman reporter with a female film crew to interview women), the transit camps and hospitals in Bosnia and Croatia should have been crowded with women giving birth to their babies or having them aborted. Yet by the beginning of this year, only three babies are known to have been born of rape victims: one of them, Emina, born in Petrova Hospital in Zagreb and abandoned by her seventeen-year-old mother, was photographed so many times by the world's eager press that the doctors had to call a halt because the camera flashlights made her nauseous.

In February last, the Save the Children Fund issued a press communiqué admitting that there was no reliable evidence to support allegations of systematic or mass rape. It claimed that so far only five abandoned babies had been identified.

Many innocents had been brutally violated. Rape is as old, as cruel and as indiscriminate as war itself. It is worth the reminder, too, that the black propagandists, the dirty tricks brigades, had been active on all sides in this war. Maybe the last word should be with those who listened to it daily, like Maja Somalot of the BBC's Southern Slovakian Service: 'This has been a very modern war and perhaps some of its events have been staged with the medias in mind.' Perhaps the first victim of rape in Bosnia was truth itself.

The allegations of systematic rape, baby farms, genocide, mass graves and concentration camps, so furiously pursued by some, so enthusiastically believed by so many, had the most devastating propaganda impact. It was the Bosnian Muslims' most potent weapon and helped make up for what they lacked in the fields of fire. The most susceptible were the Americans, including President Bush himself, which surprised many considering he had once been Director of the CIA, who are dirty trick operators *par excellence*. But the Presidential election was now only months away and Mr Bush, unpopular in the polls, could not afford to ignore the issue of human rights, especially women's rights, when the issue was being foisted so high by prominent American feminists. With a little Presidential prompting, Secretary of State Lawrence Eagleberger declared that the Serbs had committed crimes against Humanity and called for a war crimes tribunal, a second Nüremberg. He even named the criminals; two Croats, one Muslim and four Serbs. He also singled out the Serbian President Slobodan Milosevic as bearing 'special responsibility', though how he intended putting him in the dock, short of an Entebbe-style raid (and the American military do not have a great record on such matters), Mr Eagleberger did not specify.

War, the theorists would have us believe, has its rules. There are identifiable acts against civilians such as rape, murder, torture, that break these rules. (The mass killing of hundreds of thousands in Berlin, Hamburg, Dresden and Hiroshima apparently do not.) The legal precedents were set at the trial of the Nazi leaders in Nüremberg and Tokyo at the end of the Second World War and their underlying principles were endorsed by the UN in the Fourth Geneva Convention in 1949. But the Nüremberg prosecutors were helped enormously by the Nazis themselves because, characteristically, they kept meticulous records of their atrocities.

No such paper trail exists in Bosnia, Croatia or Serbia. Appalling atrocities have been committed by all three sides, even if the Serbs appear to have the edge. But finding the evidence and then the suspects would be needle-and-haystack detective work that would take the investigators well into the twenty-first century, by which time many of those who had most to fear would already have been sentenced by the Final Adjudicator. Undeterred, the UN authorized a commission of legal experts from five countries to document reported war crimes, and within a month it had compiled a list of 3000 pages of testimonies from individual victims, mostly refugees, as well as aid agencies and governments. But the dossier only confirmed what was already public knowledge, that appalling things had happened in former Yugoslavia on a scale and with a ferocity that were barely credible.

Predictably enough, after the American Presidential election was over, little more was heard from Washington on the subject of war crimes and war criminals. It was assumed that nothing more would be heard from the UN in New York. But in June this year the war crimes tribunal was announced, with a mandate to begin operating in The Hague by the end of the year. The eleven judges, among them women, would be elected by the Security Council and with true UN extravaganza they will have a staff of 373 at a cost of £13 million a year. All of this could be a trifle embarrassing. The judges may indict but they are not likely ever to convict, except *in absentia*. The charge book may be full but the dock will remain empty.

If this second Nüremberg ever comes to pass, high on the list of wanted men will be a former Serb ice-cream salesman named Zeljko Razniatovic, more infamously known as Arkan to the zealots that adored and followed him, and as the 'Baby-faced Killer' to his many victims in both Bosnia and Croatia. The UN already lists him as a war criminal. Interpol wants him on a charge of multiple murder and extortion on a warrant filed in Sweden, and the Helsinki Federation on Human Rights wants him prosecuted for the single-handed assassination of a group of intellectuals in Bijeljina in eastern Bosnia.

Arkan and his thousand-plus-strong militia, whom he calls his Tigers and who are dressed in black uniforms, played a key and particularly brutal part in perfecting the Serb pogrom of ethnic cleansing. He performed best, surrounded by his Tigers, routing out defenceless women and children with his bayonet and knife. He and his men became the most notorious of all the Serbian para-military units fighting in Bosnia, Croatia and Kosovo. After waiting for the artillery and the tanks to demolish a Muslim enclave, Arkan and his men would sweep in, forcing survivors out of their cellars, killing, looting, raping, burning. Perhaps his most infamous 'mopping-up' operation was in Vukovar in Croatia, where I saw at first hand the results of the variety of ways Arkan killed, from quick decapitation to much slower death by mutilation and disembowelment. In Bijeljina in Bosnia, he boasted how he had tied six Muslims together and then pushed them over the parapet of a ten-storey building, murdered by the hands that had once served children ice-cream cornets.

Arkan's personal fortune, amassed from pillaged towns and villages, is said to be immense. He was among the first of the war's millionaires and joked that he had grown rich on 'war surplus'. He invested part of his fortune in boutiques and a chain of ice-cream parlours, one of which is opposite Belgrade's Red Star football club, of which he is a popular and generous supporter.

Arkan believed passionately in a Greater Serbia, and in the Orthodox Church. He considered himself a decent family man and adored his own legend. 'I believe in God,' he would shout in the midst of fighting, 'and God believes in me.' He laughed the day he heard that the UN had branded him a war criminal. 'Let them come to fetch me,' he said, 'and tell them to bring plenty of body bags.' The story of Arkan, Serb, churchgoer, good husband, caring father, the ice-cream seller with the baby face, assassin and mass murderer, remains the story of the Balkan paradox.

CHAPTER SEVEN

The end of the year and nine months of war in Bosnia was approaching. Natasha had now been with us for over four of those months. On 7 October she had celebrated her tenth birthday with her first ever party and a crowd of new friends. It went famously, even if she was dazed by the avalanche of presents and all the traditional accoutrements of party-time we take so much for granted, the coloured balloons and fizzy pop, blind man's buff and musical chairs and, with a blowing of toy trumpets and drum, the entrance of a giant chocolate cake with ten tiny candles. Urged on by a dozen different shrieking voices, Natasha blew them out, closed her eyes and made her wish, and above the din of little girls running amok, she said again and again that this was her 'bestest' day. We hardly needed telling.

For an extra treat the next day she went on her first train ride to see her first feature film, Steven Spielberg's *Peter Pan*, and both enchanted her. Every day now, rain or shine, was a holiday, and she lived them at full pelt. But they were not without problems. Gradually, she had become more and more demanding, at times aggressively so. Friends and neighbours, watching her progress discreetly from the touchlines, thought it a healthy sign, proof that she was simply growing more secure and so increasingly more confident that she could make demands on us without risk. Inevitably, it was Diana who bore the brunt of this relentless insistence on attention as a matter of privileged right, Natasha taking it for granted that we were obliged to attend immediately to her whichever way her moods and fancies moved. We tried to explain as gently as we could within the limited language we shared, that we simply could not devote our entire waking day to her and her whims. Then began tantrums and sulks when she retreated into long periods of silence, often locking herself away in her room.

Another problem was that she seemed quite incapable of occupying herself. She was always yearning for company, depressed when the school day was over, when she and her friends went separate ways and she was faced with the prospect of a long gap to bedtime without them. We tried our best to fill those spaces in the evenings and at weekends by inviting a friend to stay overnight, and that led to welcome invitations in return. But it was not always so easily arranged and then she would plunge back into her dark and silent moods, not wanting our company, not prepared even to listen to our explanations. Then we too would sit and brood, wondering if she might after all have been happier staying with her Bosnian friends who were now living together in refugee hostels in Italy and Germany. Or whether, as some people had advised from the start, she would have flourished better fostered by a Croatian family in Britain. But never, even in those despairing moments, did I doubt I had done the right thing in bringing her out of Sarajevo.

In time Natasha would explain in her faltering English what we and others had already guessed. She had never been on her own before. Since she was a baby, she had grown up in a house full of other children, younger and older, girls and boys, Serb, Croat and Muslim, a large, ever-changing but always present family, playing, eating, sleeping and learning in each other's company. She had never known a time in her life when she had not been surrounded by others like herself. So it must have been a tremendous shock suddenly to find herself in a large, often silent house, without the chatter and bustle she had come to take for granted. How often, as she curled up alone, hidden under her duvet, trying not to hear the whisper of wind on the window-panes or the frightening hoot of an owl or the bark of a fox, she must have longed to hear the echoes of Ljubica Ivezic and the voices she had known so well and even loved. How abandoned she must have felt in those dark moments without them, and how she might sometimes even have blamed me for taking her away from them.

We did our best to help and it became something of a rule, when the strain showed, to let her snuggle into a sleeping-bag at the bottom of our bed. Whenever I was abroad on assignment, such a treat became a right, and I suspect there was not a little disappointment when she heard I was on my way home again. From the start, going to bed alone quickly developed into a trauma bordering at times on hysteria. We tried bringing our bed-times closer together, extending hers and bringing ours forward, hoping that in this way we could wean her into making the brave ascent alone. But despite all our cajoling and pampering persuasion, despite the companionship of a brigade of teddy bears that now shared her bed, the evening journey up the stairs was the signal for many tedious tears, petulance and stamping of feet.

Even when Natasha had exhausted us with picture-books, nursery rhymes and all the rigmarole of a child's bedtime, she embarked on what became a regular pre-sleep routine, with her own careful inspection of her room, making certain the cupboards and window were securely locked and the curtains tightly drawn, which we assumed to be a hangover from Sarajevo, when she would try to blot out the noise and sight of the night's bombardment. That over, she would spend ten times as long as any ordinary child cleaning her teeth and brushing her hair and arranging her clothes for the next morning, taking more care to smooth out creases than the most diligent valet. Then, just as we were praying that the cunning display was over, she would notice some tiny rearrangement of her room, done in the course of Diana's tidying-up, such as a book or a doll out of place, and another ten minutes would be spent, not only putting those in order but diligently checking that nothing else had been moved. After a final goodnight kiss and the last wipe of a tearful eye, with the lights out and the landing door open, we would creep downstairs hopeful that the battle had finally been won.

But within minutes we would hear a scamper of tiny feet and she would sit like a silent sentinel, hidden behind the top bannisters, ready at a second's notice to scamper back to her bed and the pretence of sleep.

We had been warned to expect traumas and psychoses galore. We had been told to prepare ourselves for more than a little naughtiness and, more seriously, nature's alarms like nightmares, hallucinations, bed-wetting, sleep-walking, sleep-talking, all of which she was certain to bring with her from Sarajevo. We were also told that she would almost certainly need therapy and that we in turn should seek expert counselling to enable us to cope. But as it happened, all she needed was a more urgent invitation from the Sandman; bed and sleep somehow had to be made a good deal more attractive to a little girl than television and chat until the midnight hour. There were many more months of fury, stubbornness and sheer bad temper before our little Bosnian finally agreed to go to bed sweetly.

Our difficulty in those months, and one we had not prepared for, was that we could not impose any degree of discipline on her, short of saying NO! She was not ours to discipline. So as we watched her confidence grow daily and her command of our language expand, we began to experience the frustration of watching a former Bosnian war waif develop into something of a pampered little girl. Fatuous as it may seem in retrospect, at the time it astonished us that someone who had so recently come from a lifetime of deprivation and not a little squalor, should now refuse to drink tap water and insist on Coke, who considered it an imposition to finish off her bread crusts, who thought it an outrage to be told to eat the white of an egg, who assumed that all meals were eaten squatting in front of the television, that children were not expected to put their dirty dishes in the sink, or their soiled clothes in the dirty linen basket, or even hang their school uniform on the hanger provided. All this from a little girl who only a few months before had taken it as life's norm to walk with buckets half a mile to the nearest fresh-water tap, whose diet consisted mainly of spinach soup and bread and who would obediently devote half her day to mopping the orphanage floors, swilling out the orphanage lavatories and bottle-feeding the orphanage babies. How easily, how readily she had adapted to the role of a privileged little girl in a comfortable home, taking so much for granted. In my jaundiced, ageing, prejudiced eye, she had become a spoilt Cinderella and I found it hard to come to terms with.

Now, of course, with the well-known wisdom of hindsight, I think I understand a little of what was happening to her at that time. She was like someone dreading the end of a perfect holiday and believing there could never be another like it, desperately, greedily grabs at every last morsel of enjoyment, trying to imprint it all indelibly on the memory. She must have persuaded herself that nothing so good could possibly last for very long, and that in weeks, perhaps even days, it would all be over and she would be whisked back to what she had almost forgotten.

What a desperate little girl she must have been at times, plagued by a suspicion never far away, that she did not and could not belong, and as with every guest in a stranger's house, there was a time to say goodbye. She had heard Vera Zoric say she could come to England on holiday until the war was over, but what did she know of the war's progress now because we had told her nothing of it? She must sometimes have prayed that the war would never end.

That is how she lived those early, fleeting and ephemeral months, and because they threatened to end without notice, she packed into their brief space what she knew her English friends had all their young lives to enjoy. Natasha had so much to lose and so much to leave behind. It must have haunted her.

She never spoke to us about it then. Her English was improving rapidly, she was a great mimic and her grasp of the vernacular and slang was remarkable. But only now has she told us that in those dark moments, when her return to Sarajevo seemed inevitable, even immediate, she would creep away to corners of the house she had made her own little hideaways and weep. We often tried as gently as we could, to coax her into telling us something of her life in the orphanage. At first there was always silence as if she had not heard our questions, or she would interrupt them and begin a conversation about something completely different. Sarajevo it seemed, was not to be spoken about; It was something to forget, to ignore, like a scar from a painful accident.

Eventually, slowly, and of her own initiative, she began to talk, though she was careful to remember only the good times. Seldom did she speak about the shelling and the suffering and the dying. Instead, she told how at weekends in winter, the children climbed the mountains to the ski slopes and made their own toboggans from fallen branches or from discarded plastic fertiliser bags, and their skis from scrap wood and string. But the summer holiday was her favourite. Then the younger children were sent off to stay with families on farms and in small villages for a week or two.

But the best thing of all, she said, was when they all came back to the orphanage and they told their stories of where they had been and what they had done, stories that would keep them talking and remembering until winter came and it was time again for the ski slope when the snow smothered all memories of summer.

'Is that what you miss most, Natasha, the summer holidays and the snow?'

'No,' she would reply wistfully. 'Most, I miss my friends.'

She had no one to share her fears with but, just as painful, no one with whom she could share her delights and secrets either. There was, after all, so much to tell. And she did need that someone because too often she felt her new world was more make-believe than real. Like Alice, she found it hard at times to believe that it was all really happening to her. Often she would ask, 'What was yesterday? What did I do? Where did I go?' as if she suspected she had dreamed it or simply wished it to be. Thankfully, it was all resolved the day she met Biba.

'This is the story of a land that died . . . and of the child that was reborn.'
Mother kisses her son's cross in Sarajevo, July 1992.

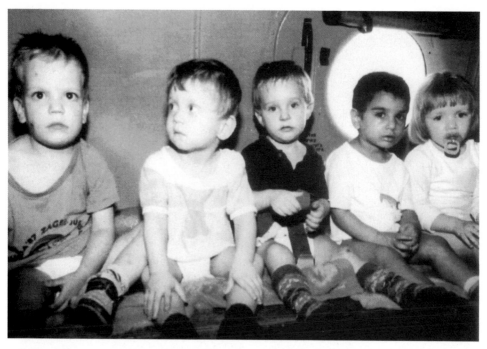

Above: 'We must save our children, only they are innocent.' Natasha's orphan friends dazed and frightened as they leave Sarajevo in convoy, July 1992.

Below: 'All had their stories to tell, personal testimonies of their captor's cruelty.' Starving Muslim prisoner in the Serb detention camp at Omarska, Bosnia, August 1992.

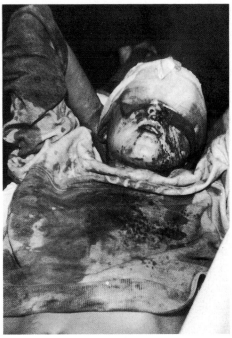

Above, left: 'Two little children, babies still, had been shot dead by snipers as a second convoy tried to leave Sarajevo.' An orphan cries behind the shattered windscreen of the coach in which Roki and Vedrana were killed, Sarajevo, August 1992.

Above, right: 'I hope the commander who ordered those guns to fire burns in the hottest part of hell.' Twelve-year-old boy blinded by mortar shrapnel during Serb shelling of Srebenica, April 1993.

Below: 'In Sarajevo there is no dignity in death.' Wounded grandmother, Ruza, carried away during a mortar attack on the cemetery as Roki and Vedrana are buried, Sarajevo, August 1992.

Above: 'Five children died, suffocated in the mass of bodies, including a three-week-old baby, crushed to death.' United Nations lorries packed with Muslim refugees escaping the siege of Srebenica, April 1993.

Below: 'A war fought with a ferocity and savagery barely believable.' A 'Chetnik' – one of the fanatical Serb irregulars that created so much terror in their random killings, rape and looting. Gorazde, Bosnia, January 1993.

Biba was an au pair living locally, a Croat from Zagreb, and having read about Natasha, eventually wrote a letter offering her friendship. They met and for the first time since she had left Bosnia, Natasha could talk uninhibitedly to another girl in her own language. They sat together in the drawing-room for an entire afternoon, interrupted only by successive trays of lemonade and cake. Biba hardly spoke a word. She did not get the opportunity. Natasha exploded, erupted, gushed like a dam bursting its seams, a breathless, non-stop, pell-mell recanting of everything that had happened since that day, that hour on 18 July when she had left Sarajevo. She told of the dancing madman, the journey over the mountains, the bonfire by the lake, the sight of the sea and the cunning of our escape . . . not a detail was missed lest the story suffered, not an incident hurried in the retelling lest the drama was lost. Biba was dragged to the pool to watch her swim, to the lawn to watch her bicycling, to her bedroom to meet her bears and see her new school blazer and even newer Brownie's uniform; to the bathroom and her ducks, to her cupboards and secret cubby-holes and all those places where her things were and which marked each part of the house as her own. Nothing was left out. Everything precious had been catalogued and everything was remembered as Natasha finally told her story.

Some days later, my youngest son William returned home from his trip to Katmandu, lean and tanned and looking splendid in his ethnic *kamise*, *shalwarz* and beads. He brought presents with him, including, to our surprise, one for Natasha. We assumed that having been hidden away in the hinterlands of Asia he knew nothing of her. But by chance in Delhi he had come across an old English newspaper with her story and her photograph. That evening she sat quietly at the dinner table, gazing with some awe at the candle-lit placings, the large leg of roast lamb and a good ration of wine with which we celebrated the homecoming of a prodigal son. It was her first sight of the four Nicholsons together and the happiness of the evening clearly affected her. Later, as she was being tucked up in bed, she suddenly hugged and kissed Diana hard. Then she said shyly; 'This good house. Me not go Sarajevo.'

By now, I was receiving a steady flow of letters, sent both to ITN and to my home, some simply addressed to Natasha c/o the Farmhouse, Surrey, which is some tribute to the Post Office. They were from all kinds of people from all over the world wishing Natasha well. Some enclosed a little money, or a photograph of the sender or a little gift. The first had arrived shortly after the newspaper stories in August and I had expected the flow to stop shortly afterwards. But again I had misjudged how a happy story endears itself to the British public and very soon there were over 500 letters and postcards stacked in date order on the dining-room table. Except for one crank (letter unsigned as always) who accused me of being a racist for rescuing a white girl when there were so many black ones more urgently in need in Africa and Asia, the writers were uniformly kind and encouraging and full of goodwill.

'Many things can wait, but not the child . . .' began one.

Another; 'I am twelve years old and I get angry when I think I live in a home and have a family when people in war do not. And they should.'

One came from a lady whose husband had recently died: 'Please don't think me a busy-body crank, I have never put pen to paper this way before . . . but my heart feels lighter for writing.'

Another must have summed up the feelings of many who watched Bosnia's misery as it was televised night after night: 'If we cease to be shocked by what we see . . . what hope do we have?'

And: 'I do wish I was young instead of being a very elderly granny because I would have done just the same as you.'

One postcard came from a man who simply signed himself 'an elderly, clapped-out tanker driver': 'Full marks but you should have grabbed a few more kids there until sanity returns.'

Another was simply signed 'an ordinary bloke': 'If they ever make you send her back to Bosnia there'll be a national outcry. I would certainly go to Heathrow and stop the plane.'

Another card with a picture of a little girl feeding ducks at a village pond, was addressed to Natasha: 'I was brought up an orphan in Dr Barnardo's Home. Now I am a granny with two sons, six grandchildren and three great-grandchildren . . . so good luck!'

One letter came too late. It read: 'I have a good friend of some forty years' standing who is a terminal cancer patient and her joy and delight over these recent weeks has been following the exploits of Natasha since her arrival in this country. I have been supplying my friend with every press cutting I can find and all Natasha's photographs, all of which have given her endless pleasure. I do not know what life remains for my friend but I do know that to see Natasha would give her overwhelming pleasure and a priceless memory to recall in her last days. Could we, between us, arrange for them to meet?'

I made contact and we began to arrange a time and a place. Natasha, of course, was to be told nothing of the reason, simply that a sick friend wanted to say hello. But a week later I was telephoned. We had delayed too long. The patient who had so dearly wanted to see Natasha, who had found such comfort in the simple story of her escape and new-found life, had died. In her last letter she wrote; 'How the story has intrigued me. It is better than any book because it is happening. I would like to have lived to see the child grow up.'

Many were letters of appeal, asking me to establish some kind of liaison or conduit between the hundreds of parentless children and babies being evacuated from Bosnia and the many families in Britain wanting to foster or adopt them. Besides the postbag, I was inundated by telephone calls to my home and my office as well as by people knocking on my front door at all hours, asking for help, wanting a first contact to begin the long, painful and frequently fruitless process of adopting a foreign child. All I could do was to pass them on to the established adoption agencies. Unfortunately, generous British charity was not matched by the British charities themselves, and as families nationwide yearned to rescue orphans from the ruins of former Yugoslavia, so the well-known adoption agencies in Britain did their best to confound and frustrate them. Overwhelmed by inquiries on how to proceed, they turned their backs. The umbrella organization, British Agencies for Adoption and Fostering, issued a statement:

> A war zone is not the right place to think about fostering or adoption. It encourages people to think of children as commodities and all too often, those who need help the most, the disabled, miss out.

If the BAAF was short on practical help it had advice in abundance:

> It is best for all children to live with their own families, in their own culture and community. Cross-cultural fostering and inter-country adoption is an option for only the few.

But there is no culture in death. Was it better for a child to stay with its family when its own community was being starved and shelled to death? They spoke of 'cross-cultural fostering' and 'inter-country adoption' as hyphenated abstractions, as if they were addressing a tired seminar of disinterested academics rather than hundreds of concerned men and women, many already with families, who were eager to help suffering people in their desperate fight for survival. The British public's concern was perhaps best expressed in a simple sentence by a mother with four children of her own but who reckoned she had room for a Bosnian refugee: 'It is time to stretch out a hand to someone.'

The BAAF response was best encapsulated by a Sandy Buchan of the Refugees' Arrival Project: 'Taking a child from former Yugoslavia is no different from any other ordinary cross-cultural fostering, and hoicking them over here is not the best way to help.'

It appeared monstrous to many of us then, that the charitable elite should pronounce so freely and with such finality in the media, as if all they said was accepted, irrefutable fact, when of course it was no such thing. There was much public hostility at their stance but they were quick to remind people of the Bosnian government's own admission that it had done wrong in allowing so many children to be evacuated, that had more to do with Bosnia's own attempts to reverse the drain of its people by ethnic cleansing than the BAAF's pet issues of inter-country adoption or cross-cultural fostering.

Aid relief agencies, household names like Oxfam and Save the Children, also appeared to be suffering from the same Bosnian blindness. The British public, ever susceptible to the nightly television war reports, wanted to help, wanted to contribute in the way it always does at the sight of others' suffering. Yet there was no obvious channel to do so, no national appeal like those that inevitably follow another African famine. In the beginning, when people's enthusiasm and generosity needed to be galvanized, there were none of the usual fund-raising telethons, no funny red noses, no hyped POP AID concerts. It was as if Oxfam and Save the Children were so mesmerized by famine in the distant Third World that they could not find time to focus on the dying on their doorstep.

Oxfam admitted that it had no experience of dealing with such a catastrophe in a developed country and had decided not to rush into the unknown and unplotted. Instead, it would give funds to the International Red Cross to administer. Only in June this year, fourteen months since the war in Bosnia began, did Oxfam send its first field officer out to Belgrade – which is not in Bosnia but a safe distance from it.

Save the Children Fund's reputation suffered from the same seeming lack of concern. Like Oxfam, it was contributing some funds to the Red Cross as well as to smaller, lesser-known local agencies in Croatia and Bosnia who knew better how to use them. But with the same lack of urgency, Save the Children waited until July 1993 before deciding to send its representative to Bosnia.

Like the politicians, the agencies looked at Bosnia and shuddered. It did seem as if the complexity, novelty and sheer danger of the crisis managed to deter two of the world's largest aid agencies from contributing directly in the war, just as it had shown up the impotence of Western governments to end it.

Under the impression that little or nothing was being done, Mr and Mrs Britain went about redressing the balance in their own way. Responding to the television images and deciding Bosnia had a poignant and urgent priority, hundreds of amateur *ad hoc* relief organizations sprang up overnight throughout the United Kingdom. It was often a single person's inspiration, or one family's, sometimes the work of a committee, sometimes the result of an entire community's enthusiasm. It was not just a matter of dropping coins into a collector's tin to ease the conscience or anonymously pledging a credit card contribution. It was one man with his own transit van collecting door to door in his own village and then driving his load of food, medicines, clothes and blankets 1000 miles or more to the Bosnian border; it was the schoolmaster in Northampton who hired a coach and drove it to that same border to pick up and bring back as many refugees as he could pack in and then went back for more; it was the retired doctor from Aberdeen, the car mechanic from Basildon, the teachers and children from a Cornish school, the husband and wife who closed their grocery store in Sunderland to shuttle their carload of provisions to Bosnia. Car-boot sales, jumble sales, fêtes, sponsored swims, hikes and bicycle marathons, door-to-door and shop-from-shop collections, all raised money, not, for once, to send to the big charities but to buy the supplies themselves and send them directly overland via Croatia to Bosnian refugees waiting on the border. Freight companies offered their lorries free, cross-Channel ferries offered greatly reduced fares as their holds filled with an Armada of charitable traffic.

Few who made the journey had any local knowledge and there were many tears of despair and frustration as well as some near-tragic endings. Vehicles were held up at military road-blocks and their cargoes confiscated because of some invented excuse. Sometimes they were simply stolen at gunpoint or their supplies were delivered to the wrong people who sold them in turn on the black market. There were many times in Bosnia when I remember coming across a British lorry or van which had been hijacked by local Croat or Serb or Muslim para-military bandits and their driver held prisoner at gunpoint, or, far more terrifying, at the point of a knife.

The International Red Cross, speaking for the other principal world-wide charities, eventually condemned the freelance do-gooders as ineffective and obstructive, of doing the least good with the maximum publicity, of being well-meaning but misguided. Perhaps it was simply the relief agencies' sour-grape response to the outsider's invasion of their monopoly. Perhaps, even though the compassion and the motivation were right, not all that was given was received.

But one thing is not in dispute. Not in many, many years had the British responded so enthusiastically, so practically and so individually, to another people's tragedy. Some were indeed prepared to hold out their hands for others to seize.

Only now did we allow Natasha to watch the television news coverage of the war in Bosnia. At first it was always done with a finger on the remote-control OFF button, to pre-empt an emotional response to worrying pictures. But we need not have worried, she showed barely any interest at all. It was as if she had decided to shut out all memory of the war and all that she remembered of it. Perhaps it was the only sensible way to cope. At any rate it was her way.

Since the start of the new school year in September, Natasha had been going daily to the local Church of England St Bartholomew's School in Haslemere. There had, at the start, been some official anxieties about her language problem, the effect it would have on her ability to stay on the learning curve, and the damage to her self-confidence if she could not keep up with her classmates. They need not have worried. Her English improved by leaps and bounds, even if there were some words, innocently picked up, we would sooner she had left in the playground.

She was welcomed wonderfully by children and teachers alike and once her novelty had worn off, she became just another pupil with a funny accent. In her first week she became school marbles champion so easily and so completely, that in order to retain her popularity, she took our advice and gave them all back. She competed in the Surrey Schools cross-country running (coming last) and the Surrey basketball competition (coming second only to a boy twice her size). She became an energetic Brownie and quoted the Brownie oath on request;

> I promise that I will do my best
> To do my duty to God,
> To serve the Queen and to
> Help other people . . .

It became a house rule that it was not enough simply to promise something to her or of her. To make it absolutely sacrosanct and inviolate it had to be a 'Brownie's Promise'; break it and you could expect the fury of God and Natasha. On Remembrance Sunday, an important date on the Brownies' calendar, she proudly helped carry the British Legion flag and of all the hundred and more little girls on parade to the town's memorial on the green, she was, I seem to remember, the only one in step with the brass band. How incongruous it was: a little girl dressed so neatly in brown and yellow, stepping out to a military tune, come with old warriors and battle veterans to remember their dead, carrying their colours, singing their hymns of war. And she so fresh from hers.

Then came what remains to her even today, her greatest achievement to date. Having never swum a stroke in her life, having never even seen a swimming-pool or the sea before she left Sarajevo a few months earlier, she won the coveted 100-metres freestyle badge at the Haslemere swimming-club gala. There was much celebration that evening, including a Chinese meal and – another first for her – chopsticks.

But there was a sad end to that day, which would have been sadder still if Natasha had seen the late ITN news. While she had been competing for her badge and enjoying the gala, Serb shells had exploded in the playground of the Ljubica Ivezic orphanage, killing four children and injuring many more. The shells had been fired at dusk while the children had been playing in the hour before supper and bedtime. Knowing, as I now do, the positions of those guns, and having seen the orphanage from those same positions, such was their range, easy sighting and accuracy, that I am certain it could not have been an accident. Natasha would have known all those killed and except for a quirk of fate she might well have been one of the little smashed bodies I watched being carried into the morgue. We told her nothing that night but oddly, when she finally went to bed, flushed with the excitement of success and not a little proud, she asked me for the very first time the question I had long been expecting.

'When will I go back to Sarajevo?'

And I could not answer. She had left that city on condition I returned her by the beginning of the new school term or at the end of the war, whichever came sooner. And the war was still a long, long way from ending.

The Serbs were now surging across Bosnia and with very little resistance. Their big brothers in Belgrade had ensured they had ample supplies of fuel, arms and ammunition as well as advisers, tacticians and weapons instructors. They had tanks and heavy artillery pieces purposely left behind for them by the former Serb-led federal army. They lacked nothing (except international goodwill) and such was their military momentum that it began to look as if they might take all of Bosnia if they wished, even if it meant reopening a second front against the Croats.

Their initial objective had always been to open up a number of crucial land corridors connecting Serbia with the main Bosnian–Serb enclaves, especially Krajina in the north-west and among them the Posavina Corridor in the north-east. But Serb ambition had grown with the ease of their conquests so that by the autumn of 1992, old fears were revived that Serbia might roller-coast on into Kosovo, Montenegro and Macedonia, in a war that would engulf the entire Balkans.

The Serbs now held over 70 per cent of Bosnia and had laid siege to many strategic towns and cities, including the ancient capital Mostar in the south-west, the industrial capital Tuzla in the north-east, Gorazde on the eastern border and Sarajevo itself. They had effectively encircled Bosnia and the land still held by the Muslims was shrinking by the day, with the UN arms embargo denying them little chance of survival, let alone recovery.

With the failure of the European peace initiative under Lord Carrington, the UN launched its own. Lord Owen, the former foreign secretary in Harold Wilson's government and a founder member of the debunked Social Democrat Party, joined hands with Cyrus Vance, one-time Secretary of State for Jimmy Carter, who had already won his spurs brokering the Serb–Croat cease-fire earlier in the year. Both Vance and Owen were considered Yesterday's Men, second runners recruited from that ever-on-standby pool of redundant admirals, generals and politicians. They seemed an unlikely couple, but then peacemakers are generally ridiculed right up to the moment they succeed. In time, the ageing Vance was to resign, tired, disenchanted but otherwise unhurt, and Owen, relishing the driver's seat, was to develop a refreshingly undiplomatic chutzpah.

Their first objective was to break the Serb stranglehold on the movement of humanitarian aid to the Muslims under siege. To that end, the UN pledged a small international army, and in September, Prime Minister Major, having solemnly pledged to

Parliament and people that he would never commit British troops to Bosnia, did another of his regular U-turns and readily agreed to send 2500. France said it would reinforce troops already there; the Canadians, Dutch and Spanish also pledged to go. The UN blue-beret army in Bosnia was now growing fast, too fast for some who warned (with that cliché for all occasions) that it would soon be bogged down in its own Vietnam. But now the UN had no choice. It had embarked on a course it could not reverse, short of ditching its original founding mandate.

In the second week of November, the Security Council beefed up its sanctions against Serbia and authorized a naval blockade in the Adriatic to prevent ships unloading cargoes at ports along the coast of Montenegro. In that week, too, the first British troops arrived in Bosnia. It had taken them three months to get there.

For the first time since the colonial sixties, British forces were on active service in three parts of the world at once; the Gulf, Northern Ireland and now Bosnia. It gave some the impression that Britannia was again straddling the globe, to others it smacked of a little bit of camouflage disguising an irreversible military decline. But to nearly half a million trapped Muslims, it meant the difference of eating or not eating, of having tents and blankets and basic medicines or suffering and dying from hypothermia, dysentery, hepatitis and those other silent killers, exhaustion and despair. In short, the British Tommy meant survival, and as if to emphasize the urgency of their mission as they arrived, the first winter snow began to fall in the mountains.

The Cheshire Regiment landed in the port of Split and drove north to the mountainous area near Tuzla in north-eastern Bosnia which was to be their area of operations. Not knowing how they would be received, they travelled in tight convoy with their Warrior armoured personnel carriers to the front and rear, covering with their 30-mm rapid-fire Rarden cannons. Those guns and some of the men behind them had seen service in the

Gulf War and many of the vehicles were as heavily tattooed as the veterans inside. The Desert Rat insignia flew from their radio aerials above the Union Jack and the blue flag of the UN.

It was a long day's drive north from the coast and when they finally and wearily arrived at their base in the town of Vitez, they passed a Christmas tree covered in snow. Hanging on it was the seasonal message of goodwill cut out of silver foil. Somebody had meant well. 'Home for Christmas' had been the cry as they had sailed from Portsmouth. But now, as they prepared camp, shivering with cold and cursing the man who had left their arctic kit back aboard the ship, every soldier knew he would not see Christmas in England. Some wondered if they would ever see England again.

The Cheshires were under the command of Lt Colonel Bob Stewart who very quickly became everybody's favourite in the media and was soon to become one of the war's most familiar faces. He appeared to have modelled himself on another legendary colonel in another very televisual war in the mid-sixties, Colonel Colin Mitchell, 'Mad Mitch' of Aden. Bosnia's 'Colonel Bob' was soon a master of the media, a connoisseur of the 'sound-bite', sometimes giving the wrong impression that the war was secondary to the television coverage of it. Newcomers were warned in the Mess that if any other officer in the regiment stole Colonel Bob's air-time, he could expect a dressing-down.

He was undoubtedly popular with his men and respected, even feared, by the local warring commanders. But his was not quite the stern, stiff upper lip his seniors in Whitehall thought fitting to the task. British officers, so it ran, should be discreet to the point of reticence and should never, ever show emotion, let alone humanity, especially on camera. That was not Colonel Bob's style.

As he frequently reminded his men, they were not in a British army operation but a British contingent of UNPROFOR, a typically ugly acronym for the United Nations Protection Force, 6000 men in all in Bosnia under the command of the French General Philippe Morillon. The Cheshires put on a brave face (and there were never any public recriminations), but it was quickly realized that they had drawn the short straw. While the French contingent had been allocated what was then considered the safer, peaceful resupply route between Bihac and Zagreb on the north-western border, the British were to patrol what had long been called the 'Black Heart of the Balkan Badlands'.

It would be difficult to find a more dangerous and treacherous terrain. From the moment they had left the tranquil river banks, the roads and tracks twisted and climbed steeply up into the mountains, routes ideal for landmines, banked by dense black forests perfect for ambush. Throughout that summer, the road between Vitez and Tuzla had been under constant attack by both Serb and Muslim guerillas, battling for control of a critical corner of Bosnia. Now that the winter's snow and ice had come early, the dangers were compounded. Not even the resident UN aid workers had much experience of operating so deep into the war's hinterland. Since the fighting had begun eight months before, only two small supply convoys had managed to get through, and with the onset of winter, they had written off all attempts to try again, even though they knew upwards of half a million people were trapped inside their enclaves.

The road through the mountains to Tuzla had been nicknamed 'Hell's Highway', and for good reason. Much of the area was no man's land, with mines scattered at random and lone, manic gunmen on nobody's side roaming at will, killing, raping, looting. One day you could touch a place on the map and say it belonged to the Serbs and the next day you would be wrong. Your guide and interpreter would confidently point in one direction and say it was safe to go there, but within a mile or two, a charred body in a burnt-out car proved it was not.

I drove with my camera crew Peter Wilkinson and Richard Berridge through those mountains from the British camp at Vitez to Tuzla. There were reports that thousands of Muslim refugees were fleeing their enclaves around Cerska, Kamenica and Srebenica, and Tuzla was expecting to be swamped by them. We were going to report the story but we were warned that snowdrifts had made the mountain roads impassable and that land-mines might have been laid on the alternative diversionary tracks. Such advice is widespread in Bosnia and if you heeded it all you would never dare leave your front doorstep. Anyway, we felt comforted by the fact that we were driving ITN's heavily armour-plated Landrover and we had snow-chains in the back. The final imperative was the story.

In normal times (and it was becoming increasingly impossible to believe there ever had been such times), the journey to Tuzla took about two hours. On that day we had travelled for five and we were not even halfway there. The warmth of the low winter sun did not touch the mountain tracks facing north, and even a partial thaw quickly froze again, creating unseen, lethal layers of black ice. Hour after hour we proceeded at walking pace, Richard and I ahead of the Landrover, guiding Peter through the banks of packed snow and sharp-edged troughs of ice, every so often watching the vehicle slide helplessly into a drift. All the time we had one eye on the black depths of the forest and the high crags of rock overhead, seeing movement where there was none, expecting an ambush at every turn; every fallen log was suspect, even the sudden flight of a bird an imagined warning.

If danger was not close about us we were not to know. But it was never far away. We could hear the sound of small-arms fire echoing from peak to peak and we sensed the mood of the small Muslim villages as we passed through them. They were still and silent and the look of fear in the eyes of the old people – because only the old remained – told us that the Serbs had been there and warned us that they would return. We know now that they did, because those villages are no longer there. Only shallow, burnt-out heaps of ash remain, and the old people who had been too afraid, too crippled or simply too stubborn to follow their families, are cremated beneath them.

This, then, was the Bosnia the Cheshires had come to tame. And they came with a dangerous, some considered imbecilic, restriction on how they should defend themselves. Under the UN 'Rules of Engagement' which governed how soldiers were to react under attack, a soldier was not allowed to return 'superior' fire if shot at. This meant that if a sniper fired only one bullet at a soldier, only one round could be returned, and it was not long before a sniper's single bullet killed the first British soldier, Lance Corporal Wayne Edwards. All governments who sent troops to Bosnia complied with the UN rule. It was meant to prevent UN troops seeming to take sides and reduce the risk of an exchange of fire becoming a protracted anti-UN campaign. But those who were exposed to fire thought it an odd way to protect themselves and eventually and secretly, the troops of all the countries present made their own law. On those occasions when a worrisome sniper hidden away in the hills had exhausted their patience, local commanders sent a few of their best marksmen out for an afternoon's reconnaissance. Or put another way, to make certain the sniper never worried anyone again.

There were other soldiers at work in Bosnia, a rag-tag bunch of volunteers who went under the collective title of mercenaries. They appeared in Bosnia once the war in Croatia was over, trying to attach themselves to elite units, usually bragging that they had fought in Africa and Vietnam. Few were ever what they said they were. Most were adult delinquents, mini-Rambos suckled on *Soldier of Fortune* and survival magazines and action videos. It was a dangerous game of fantasy.

Among them were a few genuine ex-British army regulars willing to fight for any of the three sides, depending on their political, religious or financial motives. Two were sighted by the Cheshires working around Travnik, the ancient Ottoman capital in the middle of the country. Ted Skinner, in his early forties, claimed to have been an army captain, and Derek Arnold, in his late twenties, had probably been a medical orderly at one time. Both men said they had come to help the Muslims out of sympathy and were giving them weapons, ordnance and medical training. The local Muslim commander in Travnik, Colonel

Ahmed Kulenovic, did not pay them more than they needed to feed themselves and they were given a small apartment to live in rent-free. Not surprisingly, as ex-British soldiers, they began a nodding acquaintance with the Cheshires and nothing much was thought of it. They were, in the words of a British major in Vitez, 'harmless, if a little sad'. Unfortunately for them, their casual conversations with their fellow-countrymen aggravated those they had come to help. Worse, it enraged certain other mercenaries newly arrived in Bosnia, Islamic Fundamentalists, young fanatics, mostly from Iran and North Africa.

One evening in February, a group of them broke down the door of the Travnik apartment, kidnapped Skinner and Arnold and then tortured them in the nearby village of Turbe. They were accused of passing military information to the British who, the young fanatics suspected, were passing it on to the Serbs or the Croats or both. After some hours of interrogation and some horrific mutilation, Skinner and Arnold were trussed up and shot through the back of the head. They were not the first or the last British mercenaries to be executed. Over the next ten days, six more were killed, all, according to intelligence received by the UN forces, by the same group of fanatics, probably by the same gun.

There had already been a lot of excitement, and in some quarters despair, at reports that large numbers of Islamic mercenaries, Mujahadeen, had arrived in Bosnia to fight their Jihad, or Holy War, against the Christian Serbs. It was even rumoured that 10,000 of them were training on the island of Hvar a few miles off the Dalmatian coast from Split. A BBC correspondent reported that thousands of Mujahadeen were massing on Mounts Igman and Bjelasnica and were about to charge down to massacre the Serbs and relieve the siege of Sarajevo. The story had a touch of Hollywood about it and much to the dismay of the world's press and not a few Muslims, both reports were fiction, as was all talk of the Mujahadeen Brigade. There were barely enough of them in Bosnia to make up a company and even those that did come to fight were rarely worth the ammunition they wasted.

Ever since the Serbs had begun their war, ever since the atrocities they were committing on the Muslims became known, leaders of the Islamic world had been threatening revenge and retribution. Across Arab lands, from the tops of mosques and minarets, fatwas were issued by the score. Members of the Islamic Conference declared a Holy War against the Serbs and pressed for the UN's arms embargo on the Muslims to be lifted. Encouraged, Bosnia's Muslim President, Alija Izetbegovic, journeyed to meet wealthy Arab leaders in their various capitals, begging them for weapons and cash. The Saudis and the Kuwaitis at least gave him a promise of payments in the future, which was more than he got from their neighbours. Some of the Saudi and Kuwaiti money must eventually have been received because the Bosnian Muslims have been getting weapons despite the embargo and someone has been paying for them.

It would be facile to think that the sum total of support the Bosnian Muslims received from their brothers of the faith was a few busloads of manic, zealous gunslingers in turbans and jellabas. But for the most part, in the end, Islam, despite all its sound and fury, went the way of the Christian world and shared its indifference.

CHAPTER EIGHT

'What was Christmas like in Sarajevo, Natasha?'
'People gave food and Father Christmas gave presents.'
'Lots of food and presents?'
'We had cake and I got one present.'
'And did you sing lots of songs?'
'No! No songs. We did not sing any more.'

So began another chapter in the turning of Natasha Mihaljcic's little life. Ever since her birthday in October, when she had first been introduced to a British family celebration, she had been talking about Christmas, wanting to know if it snowed as it did in Sarajevo, whether we had parties (parties had become a favourite word), did we have lots of presents (another), and most important of all, did Santa Claus come to England?

All of which was something of a surprise to us. We had suspected that in the harsh environment of the orphanage, there would not have been room for such fantasies, that the older children would have shattered them as older children everywhere like to do, that fairies, pixies, gnomes, wicked witches and the big bearded man in the red suit racing across the snowy rooftops with his sleigh, would long have been consigned to childhood's waste-bin. But Natasha believed passionately in all those things.

Every night, as I have already mentioned, she made certain that her window was securely locked and the curtains tightly drawn, the way she was told to do in Sarajevo because lights at night gave the Serb gunners a tempting target. But once she had watched Steven Spielberg's film of *Peter Pan*, once she had seen how easily the children had been whisked out of their beds by the dreadful Captain Hook and taken to the Never-Never Land, the Sarajevo habit was replaced by a very real fear of fairy fantasy. After lights out, the tiniest draught at the window causing the slightest movement of the curtains was enough to have her running to us in panic. All children grow up, it seemed, except one.

Then there was the saga of the tooth. Her few remaining baby teeth were beginning to come loose and there was some excitement when one dropped out. In Sarajevo, she told us, you closed your eyes, threw it in the air and made a wish. In England, we said, children tucked the little bit of ivory under their pillow at night and while they were sleeping the tooth fairy took it away and left a little money in return. How much? That depended on the fairy's generosity. How did the fairy get in? Through the bedroom window. Then began another tearful dilemma. Natasha was very attracted to the cash payment but under no circumstances whatsoever was she going to leave her bedroom window open at night, not even the teeniest bit for even the tiniest fairy. Eventually we negotiated a compromise. Diana would stick a note to Natasha's window-pane asking the tooth fairy to detour through our bedroom window and leave the money on the landing table. The redundant item would be waiting for her.

The following morning, very, very early, we were woken by excited squeals of delight. The tooth had gone and in its place was a shining 20-pence piece which she held high, blushing and dumbfounded by the magic of it all.

Christmas approached and as expected, Diana and I were under strict instructions to make absolutely certain that our house was on the Big Man's itinerary and that he should know in good time of all the things Natasha expected him to drop down the chimney. Her list of presents was distributed throughout the house, regularly revised and extended and redistributed again. Her Advent Calendar was pinned to the wall over her bed, and punctually every morning, before dressing, she would open a shutter and mark the date on the countdown to the Big Day.

Even so, and as always, Christmas caught us by surprise. Our family does not normally begin to put up the traditional trimmings in the house until a week before Christmas Day, but the commercialized enthusiasm in Haslemere High Street, where the lights, tree, taped carols and Rotary collection tins had been up and busy since mid-November, had confused and panicked Natasha, because it made us look rather lacking in seasonal gusto. She was furious when she went around the garden looking for holly only to find that the birds had picked off every last red berry, and dreadful oaths uttered under her breath in Serbo-Croat were directed at the man at the head of the queue who bought the very Christmas tree she had already decided should be ours. She decorated her bedroom with paper chains cut out of strips of coloured paper, insisting they should be stuck together with flour paste just as she had done in Sarajevo, and she could hardly contain her excitement as Christmas cards and small presents arrived in the post for her, many from the same people who months earlier had sent us such wonderful letters.

As Christmas Eve neared, she worked herself into a tizzy over how the Big Man in red should be received, dithering over whether she should leave biscuits or cake for him when he called, whether he drank tea or coffee, and should she leave her stocking at the bottom of the stairs or did she have the courage to hang it from her bed, which would mean *him* coming into *her* room! On Christmas Eve there was sudden panic and a rapid last-minute rearranging of furniture after Diana had absent-mindedly said that Father Christmas would be coming down the dining-room chimney. Natasha, with genuine alarm, pointed out that it was far too narrow. Thankfully, it was resolved there and then, and we made arrangements that encouraged him to land in the drawing-room hearth instead.

Late that night, after our traditional Christmas Eve party of mince pies and punch for friends and neighbours, we helped

Natasha with her final chores. Nothing, she reminded us, should hinder *his* arrival and every effort must be made to please him because he might be inclined to leave a little something extra. Natasha made the most of every opportunity! Under her instructions, we placed the telephone table prominently in front of the Christmas tree in the hall so that he should not miss it, and on it she carefully placed a letter, written in impeccable English, thanking him in anticipation for his trouble. There was a mince pie and a plate of biscuits (chocolate, shortbread, digestive and cream wafer . . . we had to admit we had forgotten his favourite) as well as an orange, an apple and a glass of milk. Natasha thought he would have preferred tea but we explained that he was not expected for at least another few hours and important men in a hurry do not like cold tea. She had thought of every last detail; even the brass fire-irons in the hearth, his touch-down spot, were pulled back so that nothing should impede a perfect landing, and she asked for a night light to be put on the mantelpiece so that he should not be delayed searching for the door. Finally, like a matron doing her rounds of the wards, she made her last checks and only then did she reluctantly go to bed – reluctantly because, as she explained, going to sleep at Christmas was such a waste of time. But for once we had an answer; Father Christmas did not visit children who are awake.

Very soon, the church clock across the village green struck midnight and like so many other millions, we began our tip-toe whispered journeys up and down the stairs, pulling boxes from secret places and piling them around the foot of the tree until all we had to give was ready to be received. Then, totally exhausted and very content, we went to bed to await the pandemonium of the morning.

Outside, our family of foxes were scampering in and out of the woods and the resident owl was on hunting trips from his oak. The night was crystal clear, the lawns already sparkling with the white sheen of frost, and the low, large moon completed the picture-postcard perfection, placing itself roundly between the branches of the cedar. Catching the first scent of Christmas magic, I wondered how long I would need to wait before I saw a tiny figure scudding across its face, getting closer and closer, larger and larger, on his way to make another of Natasha's dreams come true.

At dawn we watched her wake up to a Christmas morning. She went downstairs slowly, a little frightened, certain that nothing in the hall below was real, not the baubles and tinsel, not the swinging angels and silver stars on the magic tree of tiny white lights, not the boxes spread out on the floor beneath it, tantalizing shapes in delicious colours, not the huge stocking, blue and red and bulging, blocking her way. She dared not touch anything, it all seemed too sacred. Then she reached the table and saw her letter to *him* had been opened and she knew the moment was hers. There was the orange peel and an apple core and crumbs from the mince pie and biscuits and the half-empty glass of milk. Propped against it, he had left a card with a picture of himself and inside was a line of words, awkward and spidery and obviously written by an old man. She hugged herself and whispered them, entranced; 'Thank you for the food, Natasha, and a Merry Christmas'.

That morning there were many presents opened and many 'Gee-whiz!' and 'Oh! My-gosh-my golly' superlatives delivered in a Serbo-Croat-English mix. Diana and I felt like a pair of ageing fairy godmothers. It was not entirely our own fault. Natasha had many generous well-wishers, strangers as well as friends, and at one point in the frenzy of unwrapping, we lost sight of her completely, as she plunged into the mountain of boxes and coloured paper.

It was probably wrong to have overwhelmed her with so much, but she had, after all, published her list of presents, and who would have been brave enough to explain why some things on it had not been delivered? We had been giving to her in all things, that was her due, but it did increase her expectations, and they are, as the wise sage said, a torment! The more she saw, the greater her horizons became, the more she was given, the more she felt she should have and the more she thought it her right to receive. It was upsetting at times, but it was a trifle, and like her other little problems, it was diagnosed by those who recognized the symptoms well, mothers who had daughters the same age and were well acquainted with a little girl's self-indulgences and considered it quite normal.

After all the weeks of waiting and wishing, Natasha enjoyed every second of her first English Christmas. Our own delight in watching her was only diminished by the thought that it could also be her last. She might or might not be here to stay; her future, after all, was not entirely ours to decide. But a decision would soon need to be made.

We had by now begun to proceed with the application to adopt her. It was something that just came about. There never was any one day when we – Diana, Tom, Will and I – sat round a table and took a vote. It had obviously been our shared assumption from the start and we were now all agreed that having introduced her to a new life, we would not send her back to her old one. Better she had never left Sarajevo than be returned to it and the horrors that would cling to it all her life. So I wrote my first letter to my solicitor, formally notifying him of my intention. He outlined the various options and the principal objections, namely, in legal language, that the British court had to be satisfied that Natasha's natural parents agreed unconditionally to the adoption or that the judge was satisfied that any such agreement could be dispensed with. I was told that the entire process would be made simpler and the outcome more certain, if I could establish before we came to court whether Natasha's mother was alive or dead and, if she was alive, whether she would give her consent. I had to discover her fate or at very least prove to the court that I had made every effort to trace her.

There was scant information, but as always, my own fairy godmother waved her wand. Soon I received an unexpected letter from Natasha's cousin, Gordana Besenic, who lived with her parents, Natasha's uncle and aunt, an hour's drive from the

Croatian capital, Zagreb. In excellent English she described how she had read an article about Natasha's escape and wanted to help, and very soon afterwards, on assignment in Zagreb, I went to see them.

They lived in a pretty village close to the Hungarian border where the war had never come and where it was talked about as if it was happening on the other side of Europe. I was greeted more like a member of the family than a stranger, and was immediately bombarded with wine and plum brandy and scented tea and a table laden with home-made pies and cold sausage and the most enormous baked ham. The grandmother hobbled back and forth from the kitchen, making certain that food and drink covered every spare inch of tablecloth. Ivan, Gordana's father, was a short man with a vast girth encircled by a wide leather brass buckled belt. He clearly had a great thirst and an aversion to an empty brandy glass, both his and mine. He had the knack of filling them so that the liquid appeared to swell, unspilled, above the rim and the ability, obviously born of many years' practice, of throwing the brandy into his mouth, the way some people do peanuts. After one or two glasses, I tried to copy him and missed. But the clowning served a good purpose and very quickly we became friends and talked freely, Gordana translating. Ivan said he wanted to take me to his hunting lodge in the mountains where he would cook me hare stew and we would eat Dalmatian ham and we would drink more plum brandy. It would not matter, he said, if we could not stand because we would simply roll home again down the mountains. He said he had done it many times and he laughed aloud, great rollicking laughs which suddenly seemed out of place once he told me he was an undertaker.

Which brought us to the business I had come so far to talk to them about. Was Natasha's mother dead or alive? Gordana's mother was the sister of Milica, Natasha's mother. She told me she had not been in contact with Milica for about two years, she could not remember exactly when, it had been a telephone call, though she could not even be sure now whether it was made inside Yugoslavia or abroad . . . Milica was so often away in foreign countries that she could never tell where she was. She began by saying that Natasha's parents had been divorced but I knew this was pretence to protect the family's name, and later she admitted that she had never known the father. 'Perhaps he might have been a casual boyfriend, perhaps they worked abroad together, she didn't say. Milica never mentioned him . . . at the time the family seemed to think he was a Serb though I don't know why. It was a great disgrace to all of us when she had the baby . . . families were very strict then, they are still here in the country where the Church is strong. My mother and father disowned her, we all had to, that was the way. She never wanted the child, she told me that many times, and she got rid of it as soon as she could . . . at first we thought she had given it to a family . . . only later did she tell us she had taken it to an orphanage. I felt sorry as a sister but she never ever asked for help or money or anything. That is how she always was, on her own, doing what she wanted to do.'

She paused and reached behind her for something on the sideboard. It was a photograph of Milica. It showed a small, slight woman with dark hair and even darker, almost gypsy-like eyes, standing with that awkward, uncertain pose of someone who would rather not be photographed and is anxious to step out of the picture – someone who did not want to be remembered. I asked them if they thought I had done the right thing and they clapped their hands and said 'Yes!' I asked them if they would support me if I wanted to adopt Natasha, and again they applauded me and nodded and said that if Milica ever made contact again they would tell her of my visit and urge her to consent. They were sure she would.

Gordana's mother said: 'Milica was always on her own and that was because she was a very selfish girl who never wanted to share anything with anyone. But she is not so selfish that she would deny anything now to the little girl she threw away.' Her words, so simply put, were given greater emphasis in the slow translation and I had no need to write them down.

It was time to leave, though it was difficult to stand. I promised Ivan the undertaker that one day I would indeed return and let him take me to his mountain hideaway where we would fill ourselves with game stew and plum brandy and, like the grand old Duke of York, come marching down again. I gave my thanks and said my goodbyes but before I drove off I remembered I had brought a photograph of Natasha. It was a picture of her looking happy and radiant, about to blow out the candles at her birthday party.

Gordana gave it to her mother who took it slowly, even nervously, almost afraid to look. Then, with a glance at it and with tears already welling, she turned and walked quietly back into her house.

As was the rule now, all information I gathered was passed on to both my solicitor and the Social Welfare officer who continued to monitor Natasha's progress at monthly intervals and whose opinion, when it came to the adoption application, would help determine the outcome. Through a solicitor in Zagreb I also advertised asking for the whereabouts of Milica in the missing persons column of a Croatian national newspaper. A month later I received his reply: short of an exhaustive investigation into police and mortuary records it had to be assumed that Milica Mihaljcic was not in Croatia or that if she was, she wanted to remain anonymous.

Late in January, I returned to another assignment in Bosnia. From the port of Split, we travelled north-east towards Sarajevo, over the same mountain roads I had followed with Natasha six months before. The change shocked me. Once we had crossed the Croatian border and moved towards Mostar, the devastation was appalling. Mile after mile, village after village, was razed by shell and fire, not only those by the roadside but houses as far as you could see for miles either side of it. Thousands of acres of forests and vineyards had been burned to charcoal, it was the landscape of the damned and I had not seen destruction like it since Vietnam. But it was far, far worse than anything the Americans did there; that had been indiscriminate bombing and defoliation from the air. This was slow, methodical and selective, the planned destruction of entire communities, one by one in the relentless Serb advance, a plain of cold grey ash where once there had been a thousand sturdy brick-built homes and farms and businesses, where the enemy had never even been.

No words nor any pictures I have yet seen could adequately describe that journey north. A page or a paragraph might help portray five minutes of it, or one village, but not the extent nor the vastness nor the thoroughness of the demolition. This was not the result of close combat, of fighting house to house, floor to floor, where the only final way to rout the enemy from his shelter was to totally destroy it. This was pitiless, manic vengeance. This was not just conquering the enemy, this was erasing all evidence of him so that the land should be thoroughly and finally cleansed.

We had established our base in the small town of Kiseljak, 15 miles north of Sarajevo. For some time now, ITN like the BBC had considered living in Sarajevo to be not worth the risk. Martin Bell had only recently completed his convalescence after being wounded in the stomach and groin by mortar shrapnel, and the week we arrived, four other journalists had been hit and a photographer had survived a sniper's bullet which had passed through his neck. Once, we had all assumed that to have 'PRESS' or 'TV' festooned across your car provided some kind of immunity. Now, it encouraged an attack. It was being said that Serb marksmen had recently arrived from Belgrade who had come more for sport than politics, the sport of killing people. It was also said that they boasted of their own speciality; one targeted the head, another the heart, others preferred simply to maim. It was probably balderdash, but the story did the rounds and was believed by many, which was some indicator of the terror the snipers had now created in the city.

In between reporting for ITN, I continued my search for

Milica. I checked hospital records in case she had been among the many thousands sick and wounded and also the current list of mortuary dead. There was, as always, a large number of unidentified corpses there and I was invited to look at them. I would have done had I thought it practical, but it was not. I did not know Milica alive. I would certainly not have recognized her dead.

Helped by Dinko, my new interpreter, I found the offices of SIPAD, the construction company Milica had worked for as a cook. But it had been hit by shells and was gutted. I returned again to the orphanage, I crossed the playground and saw the shell craters where the four children had died the previous October. Only a few of the older teenage children remained, dirtier, wilder than ever, and in the dank cellar there were fifteen tiny babies, none more than three months old and all found abandoned in the city streets. The records showed only one address for Milica, the one she had given when she had herself abandoned Natasha all those years ago. With Dinko, I went to the neighbourhood but, as expected, no one remembered her, and when shells began landing late that afternoon, we gave up the search and returned to the relative safety of the UN headquarters to wait until the bombardment ended.

Towards the end of my stay in Sarajevo – it was the middle of February – I went to interview the Bosnian President Alija Izetbegovic. Very much to my surprise, while we were waiting in the corridors of the Presidency, I was recognized by the Secretary to the Cabinet. He told me that the ITN reports of Natasha's escape to England had been shown over and over again on Sarajevo television and that we had become little celebrities there. When I told him about Milica, he agreed to help and promised to place advertisements in Sarajevo's only remaining newspaper. He said it was not usual to do such a thing nowadays – otherwise the newspaper would be full of little else – but as a special favour he would speak to the editor. 'But do not expect a reply,' he cautioned. 'There is nobody in Sarajevo who does not know about you and Natasha ... nobody. If her mother does not, she must be deaf or blind or dead. And I would say she's more probably dead.'

The advertisements did appear as he said they would but to this day Milica has not answered them. Perhaps she does not want to; perhaps she is determined to remain anonymous and free of Natasha; perhaps she has married and her illegitimate child is her secret. Or perhaps, in a city where over 10,000 people have been killed, and with so many of them buried in graves marked 'Identity Unknown', Milica Mihaljcic is lying in one of them.

The cemeteries were now so full that they were burying the newly dead in old graves. Ancient stone tablets bearing miniature enamelled photographs of generations past and elaborate black marble crosses bearing plump cupid angels or hovering eagles, had been prised out of the frozen ground and dumped. Other headstones with ornate carvings and cyrillic texts were smashed and piled against the cemetery wall. Where the grave-diggers had been less than thorough or had quickly scampered to safety during a mortar attack, leaving a job half done, human bones by a newly opened tomb were evidence of the desecration of Bosnia and its people.

Before Christmas, when the Serbs had increased their shelling of Sarajevo, many among us were reporting its imminent collapse and surrender. Three months on, we were still wrong. Like the Serbs, we had underestimated the Sarajevons' will to survive. Their resistance, like their spirit, was diminished but unbroken and people were going about their business with the same dogged determination. Those who had employment went to it punctually; in a city where shells landed so often, the nearness of one was no excuse for lateness and only injury or death was a reason for absenteeism. Men and women walked an hour or more to work, sensibly following routes that kept them close to tall buildings in order to escape the mortar blasts. Yet they always arrived in their offices neatly groomed, the men in their starched shirts and pressed dark suits, the young women losing nothing of their celebrated Sarajevo chic. It was known that lipstick was fetching a higher price on the black market than coffee and dodging the sniper's round was considered no excuse for a crooked stocking seam. People treasured their civility and lived as normally as the times would allow. It was said that you could tell a man had lost his will to survive when he stopped shaving and a woman when she stopped combing her hair. It was not uncommon to pass a man in the ruins of the city, wearing an overcoat with a fur collar and a Homburg, taking his dog for a walk in the hour before dusk so that they might both be safely back in their shelter before the night's bombardment began again.

But the winter had come early and now, in February, it was beginning to bite. The biggest misery was the lack of electricity. The power stations had been severely damaged and no power meant no heat, no water and no gas and the bitter cold worked its way into every crack and cranny and froze to the bone. The search for fuel had become the day's main occupation. People pushed wheelbarrows through the snow filled with cardboard or books to burn, young boys earned a penny pulling logs behind them twice their height. Families could be seen foraging through a gutted house, pulling out the beams and floorboards. Wood was now the only fuel and the President had at long last given permission for all the trees in the city to be felled, and Sarajevo's famous boulevards, parks and leafy avenues quickly became bare-stumped wastelands. Families took it in turn to wait in the long queues at the single tap of fresh water or at the baker's for the loaf that had become most people's staple diet. The stalls in the old market-place near the cathedral were now empty boards except one that might have a single packet of cigarettes for sale, or a carton of bubble-gum, a tin of shoe polish, pipe cleaners, six clothes-hangers, or three woolly hats. Stalls that had once been laden with fresh farm vegetables were now dotted with small, neatly tied bundles of scented grass, dandelion leaves and nettles. This was what you ate to survive.

According to the UN, 240 tons of food was now reaching Sarajevo via the airlift every day, enough to feed the estimated 300,000 people there. In theory, that was just about the absolute minimum to give everybody the 1 lb 5 oz of nutrition calculated to be essential to survival. But not everybody was getting it. Much of it was going astray, at least that was the official explanation. In fact, it was being purloined by the Bosnian government to feed its army; ministers were commandeering the food, medicines, blankets and clothes that should have been going to schools, hostels and hospitals and diverting them instead to the generals.

This city had been under siege for eleven months, dependent for its survival on a precarious airlift, on an airport the Serb gunners in the hills could close with a barrage of shells whenever they wished. For nearly a year, the people of Sarajevo had been faced with the ever-present prospect that sooner or later they might be forced to surrender. Yet still they wanted to believe that international outrage at their plight would end their misery and turn the battle, that Western military intervention was only a matter of time, that the cavalry was just over the hill. But now, as they prepared to commemorate the anniversary of their year's suffering, they were numb. Anger had turned to disbelief and disbelief to despair. The West's leaders pontificated but they continued to stand aside and let it all happen. They preached that a peace could still, must still, be negotiated, trusting the promises of the same Serb leaders they had already condemned as liars and criminals.

Towards the end of February, the Serbs began their military offensive on the other remaining Muslim enclaves in eastern Bosnia. They had won so much so easily without even as much as a squeak from the people they feared most, the Americans. Their commanders openly boasted that an early spring offensive would be over by summer, and with it the war. The Serb leadership believed it had only a few months left anyhow before President Clinton was tempted to do something positive to end the war, something he had hinted at on the day of his inauguration in January. Since then, his language had been that of the euphemist and the sophist and the great pledges of the campaign were marking time or, to use a favourite American expression, sitting on the back-burner. At the time, few thought it fair to criticize him too vehemently too early; he was after all finding his feet, he was the new boy in town, and if he appeared a trifle reluctant to commit himself over Bosnia it could be seen as a wise caution, considering how the war was dividing his European allies. In the honeymoon days of his Presidency, Mr Clinton was not prepared to involve America directly in what was after all considered a very European problem. So for the time being the buck stopped there and America convinced itself that was the right and proper thing to do. From the beginning, Washington had set limits to American involvement, arguing that tragic though it was, Bosnia did not amount to the kind of 'never again' scenario that morally compelled the United States to intervene. The sensible thing to do was to convey American concern to the Serb butchers as they went about their work, but not too much to pay even a modest price in political support at home or cause the mildest diplomatic disruption abroad. So the White House spin-doctors made Presidential dithering look meaningful and indecision was dressed up as a conflict of principles. Mr Clinton had a few caustic columnists on his tail but that appeared to be the limit of national anxiety. Even the young and concerned on the campuses seemed to be busy with other things. It was a sign of the times.

In the meantime, Bosnia was getting smaller and smaller and less important and those hundreds of thousands of Muslims trapped in their enclaves were paying the price in blood and tears. Other names now replaced Sarajevo as their symbol of defiance; Gorazde, Zvornik, Cerska, Gradacac, Kamenica, Srebenica. They were all to become little Verduns.

Kamenica was the first to be broken after ten gruelling months of siege and it was a terrible taste of things to come. As the town fell and its people swarmed up the frozen mountain slopes, radio appeals from the remaining defenders said that only two nurses were left to tend the many hundreds of sick and wounded who could not be moved and who feared they would be massacred by the Serbs. Soon the radio broadcasts stopped, and then, so did the Serb shelling.

Some days after they had entered Kamenica, the Serbs invited the foreign press into the town to show what they described as evidence of Muslim brutality. It was an old routine and recognized by all who attended that day. Everyone is kept away until, in war slang, 'the garbage men have tidied up', meaning that no one would be allowed in until the Serbs had destroyed or buried all evidence of incidental outrages like shooting the sick and the wounded and silencing any who had witnessed it.

On a hilltop a half-mile from the town centre, Serb soldiers covered their faces with handkerchiefs and pulled rotting corpses from an opened mass grave. Many were headless, most had their feet tied with barbed wire. These, the Serb officer said, were forty-two Serb civilian prisoners who had been killed by the Muslims before they left. One journalist pointed out that the Muslims had gone only a few days before, yet the corpses were so decomposed that they must have been in the ground for a month or more. And many, it was noted, were wearing traces of uniforms suggesting they were soldiers captured by the Muslims in an ambush.

Kamenica was all but destroyed, much of it after the Muslims had gone. The mosque, always the first target, was a pile of smouldering rubble, and what had been the town hall was a blackened shell, its walls still too hot to touch. Within a few days, the demolition gangs would have finished their job with dynamite and a tank and Kamenica would be acres of levelled brick and timber. Within a few months of spring rains and warm sun, when the grass had grown and the weeds were at full height, nothing would show, and this once pretty, bustling town might never have been.

A few miles away, at a bridge over the River Drina, one of many that link Bosnia with Serbia, the white-painted trucks of a

UN aid convoy were waiting to cross. The convoy had brought desperately needed supplies of food and medicines for Cerska, the next small town along the road, where the people of Kamenica had fled to. But the lorry drivers knew they were in for a long wait. Ahead, towards Cerska, they could hear the now familiar booms of the guns, and when the wind turned they could smell the burning. Only when it was all over, when the gunfire had stopped, would they be invited to take their lorries forward. But the drivers also knew, because they had seen it so often before, that there would be no one in Cerska to receive them or their aid. The Serbs would explain, as they always did with a smile, that the people had not been willing to wait.

CHAPTER NINE

'Ah! Poor Michael.' It was said with the biggest sigh and the saddest face and I think she meant it. I was going back on assignment again to Sarajevo, and she was not pleased.

She did not mind me going to Bosnia because that did not mean war to her. Bosnia meant countryside and peace, and pleasant memories of warm summer days on a farm watching the cows milked and drawing unlikely portraits of pigs and chewing the juicy ends of grass in a field full of buttercups. It meant ice-blue winter skies, and snow as stiff as starch, and foreigners in scarlet clothes on ski lifts. She knew nothing of the detention camps and massacres and the ethnic cleansing that had withered her country away.

But she did know Sarajevo. Sarajevo meant shells and bullets and people without faces bleeding on the pavements, and she cried a little whenever I was bound there.

It was difficult to go and yet at the same time keep from her the horror I was going to report in that city and all around it.

'Why are you going?'

'To tell the people what's happening there.'

'The same as before?'

'The same as when you were there.'

'Fighting and lots of bombs?'

'I think so.'

'When it stops?'

'It will stop when the Serbs win.'

'Long time?'

'Soon I think. In the summer perhaps it will stop.'

'Good, then you no go again.'

'Will you, Natasha? Will you go back?'

'Never – I never go back Sarajevo.'

'You want to stay here?'

'In England yes! Always.'

'With us here?'

'I think so.'

'You only think so?'

'Yes, I only think so.'

'You have to make a decision soon, Natasha.'

'What is . . . decision?'

'Well, one day soon we will have to go to see a very important man, and he will ask you if you want to stay with Diana and me and Tom and Will and you must say yes or no. That is a decision.'

She paused, and her hand went to her raised chin, in the studied pose she adopts whenever she is about to invent new mischief. Then with her impish smile and a toss of her head she said, 'I will think. I will think of decisions. Then I tell you my decisions.' Nothing is ever a foregone conclusion with Natasha.

From that day on 'decisions' became her method of mild persuasion, changing with her mood and cunning, depending on whether she could stay up late, whether she could have friends in to play, whether we would take her ice skating or swimming, whether she could have this treat or that, and a negative response from us was bound to provoke a change of mind, another new round of 'decisions', another smile, a familiar twinkle in her eyes, another bout of mischief.

Bosnia, Sarajevo, the Congo, Cambodia, Vietnam – all wars were the same to Diana. A year after we were married in '67 I went to my first war in Nigeria/Biafra and the night flight I was meant to be on was blown up, and so for twenty-four hours she was convinced that I was dead. From then on and for another thirteen wars she has said goodbye on the doorstep half-expecting me not to return.

I was often away from home for eight months of the year, mostly abroad, and usually a long way away. My singular usefulness to ITN was to endure dangerous places, that was what abroad usually meant. But for twenty-five years Diana taught herself to be immune from anxiety, it was how she survived, and she brought up her two babies that way. For the past few years she has enjoyed her new-found freedom and independence, with our boys grown up and finding their own. She resumed what motherhood had interrupted and whether I was away or not was not essential to that equation.

But Natasha has changed that. I brought her home on the unspoken understanding that Diana and I would cope with her together, share the stress of the tiring, daily routine of looking after a little person, the stories, the bed-time theatricals, the bad tempers, the silent moods, the bad times and good, the noisy parties, the weekend entertainments. A little girl's constant demands for attention and care . . . all those things that are easier dealt with by two. A little problem shared, and a little problem is halved.

But suddenly, my going away to war or anywhere away from home meant that Diana would have to cope alone, and it meant, in the beginning at least, that she had to sacrifice her freedom and the self-indulgences that were deservedly hers. Waiting at the school gates again, morning and afternoon, was the beginning of a new circle of growing up, and with it was reintroduced all the drudgery that looking after a child demands.

There was more than a little uncertainty ahead, but Diana made her pledge public soon after Natasha had crossed her front porch and they had got to know each other in the kitchen over a glass of lemonade. To a newspaper reporter she said, 'Many things could go wrong, it's a long road, she is very vulnerable and I want to protect her. But I don't worry about me . . . I'm a tough old cookie.'

'WE MUST STOP SERBIA' was the headline in April. Hear,

Hear! could be heard faintly echoing through the world's corridors of power. How, how? was the problem. The peace plan
drawn up by Lord Owen and Cyrus Vance had now been kicked
around from one conference hall to another and was looking as
bruised and weary as the two honest brokers who were hawk-
ing it. But the more they warned of 'the only option' and the
'last chance' the more it seemed to encourage the Serbs to fight
on.

The plan divided Bosnia into ten semi-autonomous provinces, an ethnic jigsaw, with a central Parliament in Sarajevo,
which would become an open, multi-ethnic city. But most
observers recognized it as obsolete the day it was published
because the Serbs had already rearranged geography to suit
themselves, and what the plan and its two architects did not
explain was how the Serbs might be persuaded to give back
what they had won, because that is precisely what they were
expected to do. Others criticized the plan as rewarding Serb
aggression by endorsing their conquest of Muslim territory and
making the UN peacekeepers the custodians of ethnic cleansing.

Privately, Lord Owen was telling the Serbs and the Croats
that the plan need only be accepted on face-value and that once
peace had been established, any amount of horse-trading was
acceptable as boundaries were renegotiated and parcels of land
exchanged. The lines on the map were not indelible. They were,
he said, provincial and provisional. The Croats agreed to sign
because they could keep what they had grabbed, which was
more than they had expected. The Muslims, the losers, thought
it wise to do as they were told before they lost more. The Serbs
dug in their heels. They saw, as few did then, what a wealth of
murder there was in that map and how the peace formula provided the potential for even more gain. Those of us on the
ground, reporting the war, realized that far from containing
the fighting, the peacebrokers had inadvertently propelled it
into a new, even bloodier phase.

Dogged by failure, not a little ridicule, and with his partner
threatening to resign, Lord Owen began to murmur threats of

military force against the Serbs to bomb them back to reason. For his plan to work, he complained, pressure was needed, but pressure was not being applied. He reminded the doubters that his plan had to work because there was nothing to replace it, it was the only one on the table. He meant it to be a salutary warning. As the *Daily Telegraph*'s correspondent, Robert Fox put it: 'The alternative is to give the dogs of ethnic war and the hounds of tribal anarchy licence to rampage as they please.'

There were those who preached patience and caution, the non-interventionists who reckoned the Serbs were already approaching the endgame of their war and that the *de facto* partition of Bosnia was near complete. Western military intervention now, they argued, could at best only postpone the inevitable and add thousands more to the death toll. The managers of *realpolitik* in Washington and their hand-maidens at the British Foreign Office eagerly nodded their agreement. The Serbs had won, they said, or just about, and what was called for now was a little bit of diplomatic tidying-up. If there had been something of an embarrassing carve-up, then to the victors the spoils in the way wars traditionally ended in the Middle Ages, and few recent wars had been quite as medieval as this one. They argued that what was far more sensible than all the huffing and puffing over Little Bosnia, was to accept reality and enjoy the sleep of the innocent.

But war should never be the arbiter of peace, said others. They doubted whether a settlement on Serbian terms promised any peace at all. Looking over their shoulders at recent history, they wondered if Bosnia might not become another Palestine, a refugee nation with scattered Muslim enclaves, the Balkan equivalent of the West Bank and Gaza and, like them, a sanctuary for terrorism, with an embittered and displaced generation of young men and women, tomorrow's guerillas. But the non-interventionists won, and talk of military force in those early spring days was put on hold. The politicians who might otherwise have been pressed to explain their side-stepping, could conveniently excuse themselves on the grounds that nothing could be done anyway without Russia's cooperation – and Boris Yeltsin had a domestic crisis of his own to settle first, and a referendum of support to win. And the UN Security Council was promising to vote a new round of sanctions against Serbia in the hope that this time they would hurt President Milosevic hard enough to make him turn the screw on his siblings in Bosnia.

The only sanctions that had worked reasonably well so far had worked against the Bosnian Muslims, the very people sanctions were intended to help. With no independent supply routes, few generous friends abroad and no substantial arsenal of arms and ammunition, the Muslims alone had been affected by the UN embargo on weapons supply. It also denied them the right of self-defence which is enshrined in the UN's own charter but that was quietly overlooked. Both the Serbs and the Croats now had more arms than they could cope with.

To hit the Bosnian Serbs you had to hurt the Serbs of Serbia who fuelled their war-machine. Little by little, Serbia's President Milosevic was feeling the tightening of the sanction screw. Trade embargoes, the disruption of barge traffic on the Danube, the banning of international flights to Belgrade, the naval blockade in the Adriatic, all had their effect on the Serb economy and the long-term career prospects of Milosevic. Living standards were estimated to be down to 1969 levels with inflation at around 230 per cent per month. Industrial production was half pre-war levels with upwards of 70 per cent of the work-force unemployed or only part employed.

Nevertheless, the UN vote on new sanctions was an admission that the old ones were not nearly effective enough. Serbia was not prospering but it was surviving. As we had seen in Rhodesia and the Persian Gulf, where there are sanctions there are sanction-busters, and Serbia was no exception. They came by road, by sea and down the Danube. Across the borders of Hungary, Bulgaria and Romania, juggernaut convoys kept Serbia supplied with all it could afford. Cyprus became the financial conduit through which Serb currency was laundered to buy sanction-busting goods. In Greece, along the key land route into Serbia via Macedonia, the roads were packed with freight lorries bringing cargoes from the Mediterranean ports. At one border post, Evzones, an estimated 2000 trucks, including oil tankers, were crossing every day without even a perfunctory Customs inspection, all with the knowledge of the Greek government. And despite the UN naval patrol, it was hardly a blockade; freighters and oil tankers managed to slip by and unload at Bar on the northern Montenegrin coast. As ever, sanctions were leaking like a sieve.

'Thousands of women and children, the old, the maimed and the exhausted, are on the verge of dying. This is the massacre of innocents.' So began the broadcast of the Muslim military commander Sefir Halilovic from Radio Sarajevo, at the end of February, announcing the beginning of his last-ditch offensive to beat the Serbs back in the east where town after town was falling to their guns. After the capture of Kamenica earlier that month, thousands of refugees had fled to nearby Cerska. Now that too was under siege.

Within a few days, at the turn of the month and responding to the first prick of public conscience, President Clinton ordered his air force to supply aid to Cerska and other surrounding threatened Muslim villages. Every night, C130 freighters took off from their German base near Frankfurt, carrying 40 tons in 7-ton pallets of ready-to-eat military rations which they dropped by parachute from 10,000 feet. That was well above safe missile height, even if it did make the drops less than accurate, some so inaccurate that the Serbs received part of the rations intended for the people they were killing. Forty tons a night did very little to relieve the misery of the thousands trapped below or reduce the numbers of people dying, despite the USAF inspired media hype; one US network sent nine television crews and as many correspondents and producers to cover the Frankfurt operation; it had none in Bosnia.

If the skydrop did little to help the starving Muslims, it made the Americans feel a lot better. When they watched their nightly television news and saw their aircrews doing their bit for Uncle Sam over enemy skies, it helped massage the discomforting cramp they experienced whenever Bosnia was mentioned.

Within a fortnight, Cerska too was finally shelled and starved to submission and a second mass-evacuation was under way. Now, the combined mass of people from both Cerska and Kamenica were forced to trek 30 miles over the mountains to Srebenica, braving the shellfire and the landmines and the sub-zero temperatures. They went by night to avoid Serb patrols, passing the frozen corpses of those who had gone before them, and as they neared Serb-held areas, they gagged their babies and small children to stop them crying. Some, praying to their God to be forgiven, stepped over those who fell from exhaustion and left them to die in the freezing snow.

The road to Srebenica became the escape route for all those seeking refuge and it quickly became known as the Avenue of Death. Simon Mardel, a doctor with the World Health Organization, trekked it, and when finally he reported what he had seen, he was weeping as he spoke: 'I saw a lot of dead, most of them killed by shells and mortars. The shrapnel wounds were horrific . . . too horrific to describe . . . headless, faceless people, limbs torn off. I saw a foetus of about eight months spilled out on the road by its dead mother. I have been to Ethiopia and Liberia and Afghanistan . . . but I have never ever seen anything so ghastly.'

Srebenica had been a lively little market town tucked into the side of the hills overlooking the Drina valley. For ten months it had been cut off and the roads into it mined, with Serb snipers hitting anyone who dared move beyond the cover of the buildings. But somehow it had survived. Now it became the next target on the Serb artillery hit-list and as soon as the guns were in place in the mountains around it, there began a fortnight of constant shelling so thorough and so accurate that nothing and no one was untouched.

The pre-siege population had been 6000. Now it was 60,000. There were 2000 sick and wounded, 300 of them critically. At the hospital, Dr Ejub Alic said that he was carrying out operations and amputations without anaesthetics, patients, including children, were just strapped to the table and wadding stuffed between their teeth to stop them biting their tongue off. He said there were no medicines left, no bandages, not even soap. Hospital laundry was being done in the river and left on the bushes to dry and sometimes the Serb machine-gunners cut it to ribbons for their amusement. At night, men and boys crawled through the fields into no man's land to forage for maize or the roots of wild plants, or berries. Sometimes they came back with food. Sometimes they did not come back at all.

As stories of Srebenica came trickling out of Bosnia and as the television reports by the British combat journalist Tony Birtley were broadcast world-wide, the little town became a three-cornered symbol of Serb atrocity, Muslim defiance and Western impotence.

One man in the midst of it made his own symbolic gesture. The Serbs, now completely surrounding the town, refused to allow any UN aid convoys in or any of the civilian sick out and no amount of pleading could change their minds. So General Philippe Morillon, the UN commander in Bosnia, decided that to highlight Srebenica's terrible plight, he would make his headquarters there. Many thought it the reckless act of a stubborn old man which would damage the UN's neutrality. It might also partly have been an act of penance for a foolish assessment he had made earlier when he visited the town and said he had found no evidence of atrocities there. Whatever the motive, his dramatic move achieved what he had intended, focusing attention on the stalemate that was killing people by the score. As long as the Serbs refused to let supplies through, General Morillon would stay. That weekend he broadcast on the local radio: 'People of Srebenica, fully conscious that a major tragedy is taking place, I will remain to try to calm the anguish here and try to save you. Do not be afraid. I will stay with you.'

It was theatrical. It was a gamble. It could have cost him his career and consigned him to the waste-bin. But it worked, more or less, and those who had thought him ridiculous ate their words. The Serbs agreed to let the convoys through and allow the empty lorries to bring out the women and children and the sick. A ceasefire was agreed and that night, what was left of the ruins of Srebenica's main thoroughfare was renamed General Morillon Street.

But the nightmare task for the brave and tireless people working for the UN High Commission for Refugees was not over. Indeed, it was just beginning. Local maverick commanders erected their own road-blocks and demanded food and fuel before they would let the lorries pass, and enraged Serb women formed human barricades, attacking the civilian volunteer drivers with axes and scythes, smashing their windscreens, screaming and spitting at them for taking sustenance to the enemy. There was worse to come. A few days later, as a second convoy prepared to leave Srebenica in open trucks packed tight with refugees, things went terribly wrong. The town's Muslim leaders suddenly and unexpectedly refused to let them go, accusing the aid workers of assisting in the Serb's ethnic cleansing by evacuating so many civilians. Without them, they argued, there would be nothing left to defend; emptying the town was tantamount to surrender and surrender was never an option. Eventually, they agreed that this one convoy could leave but it would be the last, they said.

As word went around, the thousands who had congregated in the town's centre now stampeded the lorries, breaking through the cordon of aid workers. They pulled people off, throwing the old and the very young to the ground, fighting for space. The same people who had clung together for ten months to survive the siege, sharing all they had, including their suffering, now clawed at each other's faces and trampled the weaker ones underfoot in the hysteria to escape.

When it was over and the last of the lorries had gone, two little bodies lay crumpled in the snow. By the time the convoy reached Tuzla, two hours later, five more children had died, suffocated in the mass of bodies, including a three-week-old baby that had been forced out of his mother's arms and crushed under foot.

As the UNHCR regrouped and reorganized its land-aid corridors, an airlift was underway. Royal Navy helicopters and French Pumas began an air shuttle between Srebenica and Tuzla, carrying the sick and wounded. On the first day, 130 people were rescued this way without interference from the Serb guns. But it was not to last. One morning in mid-April, as the helicopter crews were loading their human cargoes from the football field in the town, Serb shells landed in quick succession. Two Canadian soldiers were wounded and crawled aboard the last helicopter as it made its rapid departure. It would be some time before they returned. The air bridge was suspended.

Then followed the most intensive bombardment of Srebenica since the siege had begun, though no one in the UN force could explain it. It was said that the Serb leadership in Belgrade was infuriated by American and Russian threats to use force against them. Dr Radavan Karadzic, leader of the Bosnian Serbs, the poet and one-time practitioner in psychiatry whose own efforts at black propaganda had become the sick joke of the war, announced that his soldiers were not to blame for the shelling and that Muslim was firing on Muslim to provoke international outrage. Only a week before, Dr Karadzic had sent a personal letter to individual members of the UN Security Council in which he promised that his forces would 'freeze all military activities around Srebenica. Muslim civilians are free to stay or be evacuated, in both cases they will be protected. Serbian authorities guarantee ground and air corridors for aid purposes or evacuation of the sick and wounded, and UN helicopters are free to perform their humanitarian functions.'

On 12 April, the second day of the Serb bombardment, with Dr Karadzic still insisting it was not happening, seventy-two people were killed in the town, among them fifteen children. Louis Gentile, an aid worker, witnessed it:

People were throwing bodies into ox carts or wheelbarrows or anything that moved. I say bodies, because some were just about alive and some were not. Some did not look like people anymore, they were simply parts of people. The shells landed right down the middle of the main road – they call it General Morillon Street now – and clearly they were meant to kill as many as possible. Other shells landed where children were playing football . . . that is where most of them died. One, he must only have been about six or seven, I saw his body. Some yards away I saw his head.

UN relief coordinator Larry Hollingsworth was also there:

I hope the commander who ordered those guns to fire burns in the hottest part of hell and I hope the soldiers who fired the shells have nightmares forever more and their sleep punctuated by the screams of the children and the cries of their mothers.

The suffering of Cerska and the images of Srebenica had become scars on the television screen and Bosnia suddenly loomed large again. The two names dominated every news bulletin on every channel almost every day and the newspapers were filled with their stories of survival, suffering and death. Politicians and commentators alike contributed new phrases to the vocabulary of outrage. Members of Parliament frantically waved their question papers at Madam Speaker for a chance to express their indignation. Some demanded if the Prime Minister would do anything to stop the Serbs capturing Srebenica, when everyone knew he could do nothing, even if he wished to.

It was the previous occupant of Number Ten who seized the moment and launched her own offensive in her old familiar way. Baroness Thatcher, at her most bellicose, accused the British and other governments in the EC of being 'accomplices to massacre'. She said: 'This is happening in the heart of Europe and we are doing nothing to stop it. I am ashamed.' She continued her war talk and the chastisement of those she now privately called the 'plasticine men' on American television; 'In the Falklands war we defeated a dictator. We had the weapons and the will. Today, over Bosnia, we have the weapons but we do not have the will.'

Members of the British Cabinet quickly closed ranks and formed a thin blue line against the Iron Lady's assault, describing her as 'wild-eyed' and 'emotionally unstable'. They pointed out that Britain had contributed £70 million in aid to Bosnia and what else could be done, short of a unilateral, suicidal invasion? But they knew, as the country knew, that she had said exactly the right thing at the right time. She had struck a chord, and the Prime Minister, despite his anguishing at the Dispatch Box, would ignore it at his peril, or so it was hoped. What was certain, was that one day, when he and his European cohorts had to explain away their paralysis, they would not be able to say they knew nothing of Srebenica.

There was much hand-wringing, heart-searching and second guessing by European leaders, mesmerized by European Unity, unable to agree how to end a war on their doorstep. Their generals twiddled their thumbs, played their computer war games, added up the arithmetic of a military solution and shook their heads at the cost. They were at a loss. Nothing made any military or political sense. There was no common denominator. Nothing balanced. Only yesterday, conventional wisdom had declared nationalism outdated, the integration of nations inevitable and a European war inconceivable. The Bosnian equation had turned the theory on its head and the periodic eruptions of public and political outrage were followed by fearsome assessments of the military consequences of intervention and a general cooling of enthusiasm. Srebenica was described as the final act of the Bosnian tragedy. It was not. There was more to come – many, many months more. And more Srebenicas.

War raged on the diplomatic front. In the last days of April, the UN Assembly voted as expected on a new round of sanctions against Serbia, which included a total ban on all trade by land, sea and air, a world-wide freeze on all assets of the Yugoslav 'rump', that is, Serbia, Macedonia and Montenegro, and the seizure of aircraft, ships and vehicles found on foreign territory.

Potentially the most effective new measure was the agreement forced upon the Greek and Turkish banks in Cyprus to close the financial loophole that for over a year had allowed millions of pounds of Serbian money to be channelled through the island, beating sanctions by paying Cypriot front-men enormous commissions to buy on the world market all that Belgrade wanted. It was a sad day for the Serbs, sadder still for the Cypriot bankers who threw up their hands in protest, pictures of maligned innocence, denying all knowledge of transactions that had made so many of them millionaires.

Condemned as the pariahs of Europe, their foreign bank accounts frozen and their borders sealed, the Serbs were encouraged to revalue the support they were giving their brothers across the Bosnian border. On the last weekend in April, President Milosevic unexpectedly appeared on Belgrade television. For more than a year, he had used his favourite medium to bolster support for the Bosnian Serbs, but now the words on his teleprompt were altogether different. He also sent a letter by special courier to Pale, the headquarters of Dr Karadzic, the Bosnian Serb leader, and in it he warned his old drinking and gambling partner (to name only two of the vices they shared) that either he signed the Owen–Vance peace plan or the supply of fuel and food would cease. Dr Karadzic understood perfectly. Within a week of the new sanctions being announced, Lord Owen received a request from Milosevic to fly to Belgrade for an urgent meeting, and two days later on 2 May, in Athens, Dr Karadzic, shaking his grey mane in disbelief and muttering the words 'coercion' and 'blackmail', put his name to the document that promised to end the war. There was to be a ceasefire, followed by the retreat of all armies and their heavy weapons to agreed lines and the quick dispatch of a large UN force – upwards of 25,000 men, including Americans – to supervise and enforce the peace.

Lord Owen was jubilant. Nearly five months of bickering and deceit were over, or so it appeared as he stood in front of the world's television cameras under the hot Greek afternoon sun. Now he could shame his critics and laugh back at those who had ridiculed him and censored him as being erratic, impudent, offensive and most un-English. Now he had the three signatures on his piece of paper, now the real negotiations could begin, sans howitzers, sans mortars, sans ethnic cleansing. The map of Bosnia would be redrawn by consensus. When the cheering subsided, it did seem eminently reasonable. But that evening, Lord Owen had barely had time to change for the celebratory dinner, when the cards he had stacked so painstakingly threatened to come tumbling down. Dr Karadzic, as he boarded his private jet to return to Bosnia via Belgrade, had answered a reporter's question by saying, almost as an afterthought, that his signature meant nothing unless it was endorsed by his Bosnian Serb Parliament in Pale. And his parting words as he climbed the steps to the waiting tumbler of brandy implied that there was no guarantee it would be. It was another Karadzic dance; one step forward, two steps back, and would have smacked of farce had it not been so much a tragedy.

Lord Owen put on a brave face. Western leaders followed his example, even persuading themselves that Dr Karadzic's signature was all that was necessary because nobody outside Bosnia recognized the so-called Parliament. But they failed to see or, more likely, they deceived themselves, that it was not possible to accept the authority of the leader of the Bosnia Serbs if you rejected the assembly that elected him.

The night before the Bosnian Serb Parliament in Pale met to vote on the peace plan, local television newscaster Risto Djogo read out world news reports calling for immediate military intervention, specifically American bombing attacks, if the delegates did not ratify the plan. Still on camera, Djogo took out a pen and paper and scribbled a quick note, then he pulled a revolver from his pocket, put the barrel to his temple and squeezed the trigger. To the sound of a loud explosion the screen went black. Moments later the picture returned, showing a bloodied Djogo slumped over his desk. Then he lifted his head, wiped away the fake blood and said: 'Ladies and gentlemen, it is not suicide to sign the peace agreement. It is suicide not to sign it.'

Risto Djogo's bravura was lost on his compatriots. When the delegates met in a ski chalet on Mount Jahorina overlooking Sarajevo, known in the pre-war tourist brochures as 'Happy Valley', they rejected the plan almost unanimously. But, like the good democrats they pretended to be, they agreed to put it to the people in a referendum. The date was set for 15 May, but it was a charade and foregone conclusion and everybody knew it.

President Slobodan Milosevic had come all the way from Belgrade to persuade them to do it his way but to his shock, because they had never questioned him before (he was after all their quartermaster), they ignored his advice and his threats. They were defiant.

'We are fighting Islam.'

'Better American occupation than Muslim.'

'Accept the peace and we've sacrificed our young for nothing.'

They spoke as if they expected history to pass judgement that day, shouting and chanting like evangelical revivalists, appealing to God, appealing to their past to guide their future. The soldiers guarding the entrance wore brand-new caps and uniforms and carried newly polished rifles and sang century-old songs of war against the Ottoman Turks.

There was a smell of suicide in the air, and a humiliated President Milosevic swore obscenities and described them as drunken poker players throwing everything away on a wild gamble: 'There is no alternative to peace and from now on every Serb death will be in vain.' This from the man who had come to power selling the Greater Serbia dream, the man who alone and for his own ambitions, had engineered the war in Bosnia and had urged people to kill for it.

He had become Frankenstein no longer in control of his

monster, the master tactician who had finally over-stretched himself, now whistled at and jeered and called a traitor by the same people who had once hailed him as Serbia's salvation. He suspected Dr Karadzic of double-dealing but it was not the manic doctor with a penchant for lying who had won the day. It was his military commander, General Ratko Mladic. He was the third strongman in the Serbian unholy Trinity, the man they called the Serb Napoleon.

The plump little General with the unsmiling face was the man who had defeated the Croats and levelled Vukovar and had ordered the massacre of 200 or more wounded Croatian prisoners of war as they were being taken from Vukovar to Zagreb, having guaranteed their safe passage to the International Red Cross. He had laid siege to Sarajevo and his words had been heard over a field radio: 'Bomb them, shell them, blast them, don't let them get a night's sleep ... there aren't many Serbs down there.' It was General Mladic who had masterminded the pogrom of ethnic cleansing and ensured it was carried out with thoroughness and vigour. It was he who had sent so many thousands to the detention camps and, if he had not personally sanctioned it, had turned a blind eye to the rape of so many women prisoners there. He was the officer who had ordered the shelling of Srebenica, the man Larry Hollingsworth hoped would burn in the hottest part of hell. The General had always insisted that his war was not a simple land grab but a greater Serbian struggle against the combined international forces of Fascism and world Zionism as they tried to destroy the Christian Orthodox Church. He warned of a covert Vatican plot to undermine Serb culture and the dangerous rebirth of the Austro-Hungarian Empire, which he said was being masterminded from Bonn.

All of this could have been dismissed as ridiculous had Mladic not so fervently believed it; as sad and inconsequential had he not been the man who, as supreme commander of Bosnian Serb forces, could wave a finger and condemn thousands to slow starvation or hundreds to an immediate death. When the history books are written, he will be recorded as one of the most, if not the most, pivotal figures of the war. He has already been branded by the Americans as the number one war criminal. When he was warned that the Americans might bomb his forces, he laughed: 'If they bomb me, I'll bomb London . . . we have the Serbs, we have the dynamite.'

The General's impassioned speech to the assembly in Happy Valley carried the day and, satisfied with the result, he left to resume his war. Clearly not impressed by appeals for calm, he ordered that the bombardment of Sarajevo be resumed, and ordered, too, the destruction in the occupied town of Banja Luka of two sixteenth-century mosques, the Arnaudija and the Ferhad Pasha, considered among the finest in the world. He was ruthless, erratic, emotional, aggressive, moody and sometimes tearful. It is quite possible that General Ratko Mladic was also mad.

> It's time for action.
> Send in a battalion of Think Tanks.
> Air Drop a Study Group.
> Launch a sub-committee!

It was a *Time* magazine cartoon by Walt Handelsman showing President Clinton poring over a map of Bosnia, surrounded by his generals. It perfectly summed up both the dilemma and the inaction. What now appeared to be the terminal collapse of the peace plan brought the new young President face to face with the promise he had made in the election campaign and one he had dodged ever since; to so something positive to bring the war quickly to an end.

In the beginning, he had sat back hoping sanctions would do the job. Then, instead of backing the Owen–Vance peace plan, he effectively sabotaged it by not giving it his unqualified support. He then proposed lifting the UN arms embargo and giving weapons to the Muslims, in effect levelling off the killing fields. Then, after the Athens débâcle, and taking up Lord Owen's option, he proposed clinical air-strikes on selective Bosnian-Serb military positions and supply routes. In return, he pledged upwards of 25,000 GIs as part of a UN peace-keeping force in the unlikely event that peace would break out.

Having announced his plan in advance, he then sent Warren Christopher, his ageing Secretary of State, on a ride around the capitals of Europe canvassing support. He did not get it. The British, French, Germans and, more importantly, the Russians, were not even lukewarm. The President, they said, was badly advised, and Mr Christopher had not done his homework. Dropping bombs on the Serbs could have only a limited effect, even a counter-effect, given the ferocity of anticipated Serb retaliation. The Americans were reminded that not even their extensive B52 carpet-bombing in Vietnam had won them their war there; nobody could remember when air attacks ever had. More important, the Americans were told not too gently that there were over 6000 UN troops on the ground in Bosnia, mostly French and British, escorting vital humanitarian aid, and what did Mr Clinton suppose would happen to them and their aid once his bombs exploded? Would the Americans be as keen if they had men there too? Would they be brave enough to put in ground troops before their air-strikes?

None of this much pleased the President. Men who sit at the desk in the Oval Office are used to getting their way on international affairs, in keeping with the American belief that every foreign policy decision is America's gift to humanity. Suddenly – and it seemed to happen overnight – the transatlantic rift edged wider and presidents and prime ministers on both sides of the Big Pond retreated to their cabinets exasperated.

For months, Mr Clinton had been criticized by his European allies (a term used loosely now) for not providing a lead. Desert Storm had after all set a precedent, with America the world's policeman, protector of the New World Order, and every dictator on notice to quit. Now President Clinton had made an initiative and he rounded on those who rejected it.

A frenzy of sniping from behind the White House shutters began. European leaders were called 'wimps' and President Clinton, suddenly less than his urbane self, likened them to a family living in an upstairs flat, smelling smoke on the ground floor but refusing to call the fire brigade for fear of damaging the stair-carpet! Mr Major was lampooned as 'Mr Wobbly' and described by one of New York's most trenchant columnists as 'being just about as strong as vanilla'. Jo Biden, a leading Senate hawk, had heads nodding from coast to coast, when he said that the European inaction over Bosnia was 'a discouraging mosaic of indifference, timidity, self-delusion and hypocrisy'.

After one entire year of his own indifference, it did appear as if Uncle Sam was raring to have a go. But what many suspected was really happening was that President Clinton's friends were now cunningly trying to inoculate him against charges of breaking faith with his campaign pledges and to prove he was not the paper tiger so many were beginning to suspect he was. Presidential indecision, it seemed, had ended. To his mind, to bomb or not to bomb was no longer a question. The question was when.

His agonizing had been acute and visible and there was some sympathy for him. This was not the kind of crisis any new President should be confronted with, especially one so young and inexperienced, desperately searching for the magic formula that would unite his fractious advisers, win the support of Congress, satisfy the timid Europeans and stop the slaughter. On that May Day weekend he thought he had found it and had gone wholeheartedly for the military option – bomb the Serbs to submission (if not back to the Stone Age). And this from the man who, as a student in the 1960s, had scorned the Vietnam War and had crusaded against it from the comfort and safety of his Oxford college. There had been a remarkable reversal of roles. Those in the administration, Congress and the media who had always been against military intervention anywhere for any reason, were now rooting for the military muscle. And the generals who lived by the rule that only force deterred, had become the doves. The American military's doctrine of overwhelming force, without which they would never leave their shores, now gave way to an overwhelming reluctance to get involved. And for once the generals had the American public on their side. Not only did the polls show a general dissatisfaction with the way the President was handling his first foreign policy crisis but confirmed that Mr and Mrs America were not prepared to have their sons' and daughters' blood spilled in a faraway place for people with unpronounceable names. Air-strikes, maybe! GIs on the ground, never!

The use of hi-tech air warfare has had a superficial attraction to all politicians since the Gulf War. Selective attacks, accurately, devastatingly delivered, promised the low risk of returning body-bags. But it ignored the findings of the Gulf War post mortems in which the US Air Force and Navy admitted what a rotten job they did. Half their pilots failed to find their targets, wasted half their bombs on the wrong targets, and in more cases than was credible, killed their own people on the ground. It transpired, from the evidence submitted, that the laser-guided bombs we had all seen on television disappearing down chimneys and Tomahawk missiles cruising along highways in Baghdad, had been less than half the truth. It did not encourage many to believe that American pilots would do any better in the steep mountains and deep valleys of Bosnia as they searched for Serbs to kill.

There were optimists, like Captain Charles Moore of the US aircraft carrier *Theodore Roosevelt*, sailing his ship 50 miles off the Dalmatian coast and carrying the F18 jet-fighter bombers that would be used in an attack: 'If we got up before breakfast we could knock out one helluva lot of Serb artillery sites before lunch.'

NATO Intelligence briefing papers were not so sanguine. To attack specified ground targets, especially with laser-guided bombs, might require men on the ground to provide the beam if secondary aircraft could not because of the terrain. They even questioned the effectiveness of American fast attack aircraft like the F18, the right choice in the Kuwaiti desert but not perhaps for the geography of Bosnia. The one aircraft that could be used was the A10 Warthog, slow-flying, highly manoeuvrable and with a 30-mm cannon that could knock out a tank. But it was also highly vulnerable to small-arms fire and there would certainly be American casualties. A five to one ratio was suggested. It was also remarked that the announcement by the American military now to allow women pilots to fly combat missions was peculiarly ill-timed, considering they might be sent into action against the biggest assembly of mass rapists since Russian troops entered the ruins of Berlin.

But the Pentagon war-wheels had already begun turning, despite the doubts of its Chief of Staff General Colin Powell, and the war-game scenario was computer-programmed with Intelligence information gathered by its spy satellites and its spies on the ground. The plan seemed simplicity itself, even if its core assumption was questionable, which was that even though the Bosnian-Serb forces were well stocked with arms and ammunition they could not sustain more than a few days of concentrated bombing. Aircraft would attack military and civil headquarters, followed by the communication systems. The army would be quickly immobilized by destroying fuel dumps which had already been located as well as supply roads and bridges and any army convoy seen on them.

The Bosnian-Serb army was organized into seven Corps, each with its own headquarters, the sites of which were also known. Under the Corps' command were roughly 115 combat and combat support units, all of which had their own vehicle parks, fuel and ammunition dumps, 400 in all. Most of them had been identified by American reconnaissance aircraft. If the Serbs retreated with their vehicles and artillery into the forests, infra-red sensors would seek them out and artillery batteries and infantry units alike would be terrified into surrender by napalm, fuel air explosives and cluster bombs. It was confidently predicted by the game planners that the Serb army of

150,000 men would rapidly desert and disperse and be reduced to rag-tag demoralized mountain bandits capable of little else but sniping and sabotage.

Giving the impression that the generals on both sides of the Atlantic were ignoring the bickering that was going on among their politicians, NATO then unveiled its plan for the specific deployment of a peacekeeping force once the Americans had forced the Serbs to wave the white flag.

Seventy-five thousand troops would be involved, the largest force since NATO was founded. America would contribute 30,000, Britain about 10,000, including a full brigade with Challenger tanks. France, Spain, Sweden, Canada, Belgium and Holland would also contribute, and the Italians would provide a field hospital. It was hoped that the Russians would honour an earlier pledge to send troops, even if, as they had insisted, NATO paid for them. Britain already had a squadron of Tornadoes at a base in southern Italy, and the aircraft carrier *Ark Royal*, with its Sea Harriers, was patrolling the Adriatic.

Then, on the weekend of 8–9 May, NATO staged a naval and air exercise off the southern coast of Portugal. More than sixty ships were involved and over 100 aircraft. Perhaps, people were saying, all the political squabbling was just a smokescreen. Perhaps the military option was really on and President Clinton was about to send his planes to bomb the Serbs back to reason.

By midweek, the 82nd Airborne Division had been placed on alert at their base at Fort Bragg, Texas. In Europe, 250 American fighters and bombers at their bases in Italy, Germany and Turkey were put on standby. In the Adriatic, American warships closed around the carrier *Theodore Roosevelt* and as he strolled across the lawns of the White House Rose Garden for another of his informal outdoors Press Conferences, President Bill Clinton let it be known to a colleague that he was free to pass on to his favourite journalists a remark he had made in Cabinet: 'This is about the time we turn up the heat.'

That same day, an advertisement appeared in the *Commerce*

Business Daily, which went almost unnoticed. It read:

> Urgently required, approximately 125 linguists in Serbo-
> Croat to provide translation and interpretation support to
> US forces in Yugoslavia to be assigned in the first instance
> to base camps in Sarajevo.

Full insurance of loss of limbs or life was guaranteed – what the
Americans call 'dismemberment cover'.

CHAPTER TEN

So began the final chapter. For Bosnia it was the beginning of the end and for Natasha, child of Bosnia, it was the end of the beginning, the start of a new life with the promise of a new name. Soon she would be preparing to celebrate her first year in Britain as part of a family with the prospect of becoming a British citizen.

These early months of her new life with us had been a wonderful example of how easily, comfortably, even nonchalantly, the British absorb foreigners who come to stay. How confident she is now, how exultant, how precocious, canny, contrary, capricious, happily adapting, eager to learn. As I write, I have her first year's school report in front of me, the first school report that, after all the years of educating two sons, it is a joy to read!

Natasha is extremely diligent, conscientious and highly motivated. She listens attentively and communicates confidently and is developing an excellent vocabulary. She has a natural aptitude for mathematics and understands new concepts quickly.

RELIGIOUS EDUCATION: Natasha has been encouraged to show love and to respect others.

HISTORY: She has shown great interest in finding out about invaders and settlers.

PERSONAL PROGRESS: Natasha is an extremely happy, lively little girl with an endearing sense of determination. She prefers the company of a select group of friends who have been loyal and supportive. She deserves the highest praise . . .

These twelve extraordinary months have seen her trans-
formed. Who would recognize the war waif now, the thin and
timid girl born Jelena Mihaljcic, registered orphan number 388,
domicile Ljubica Ivezic, Sarajevo, of no great expectations? And
what was there now to recognize of the land she had left at the
end of the war from which she had escaped?

The siege of Sarajevo was barely four months old when I
took her away and everyone there was expecting it to be over
quickly, just as soon as a sympathetic world outside understood
their suffering, just as soon as it realized what was at stake.
They had listened to the West preach the sanctity of international law and believed it when it threatened retribution
against those who wanted to settle ethnic and territorial griev-
ances by war and purge. America and its allies had done it to
Saddam Hussein. It could only be a matter of time, weeks perhaps, before they did it to the Serbs. That is what everyone in
Sarajevo believed then. Bosnia believed it.

WASHINGTON ABANDONS BOSNIAN MUSLIMS

VANCE – OWEN DREAM SHATTERED

SERBS CELEBRATE END OF MUSLIM STATE

The newspaper headlines chronologically heralded what was
presumed to be the ending of the war. Most certainly, it was the
death of a nation.

Two weeks before, sabre-rattling President Clinton was
about to turn up the heat. Now, in the last days of May, he
was cooling it again. America and Europe were friends once
more, the rift had been repaired, special relationships had been
renewed and Bosnia was the sacrifice.

The generals in the Pentagon and at NATO headquarters in
Brussels were told to put away their war plans and mark time,
and President Clinton, continuing five months of muddle which
mirrored two years of European floundering, did as he was told
by the same European leaders he had only weeks before called
wimps and wackos and announced that he would do nothing.

After all the preparation, the military alerts, the aircraft on standby, the Marines packing their kitbags in Texas, the search for 125 Serbo-Croat speakers, despite the Presidential nod and a wink, the military option was off. In the awful officialese of the White House, the Bosnian policy, for that is what they dared to call it, was . . . 'put on hold'. Unable to persuade his allies (and the word was being used again without embarrassment) to endorse his use of air strikes against the Serbs and unsure, anyway, how he could sell it to Congress or Country, the President abandoned his high moral stance and took a breather on the Balkans.

It could not last long. The Americans would not forgive the Europeans, especially Britain, for the way they had so publicly rebuffed and humiliated their President at a time when he was in need of their cosseting and some diplomatic massage, and they would find a time to avenge it.

But the raw President, determined to get something right, still clung to the other straw, his other option to re-arm the Muslim . . . to level off the killing fields. Soon he was to offer it again, this time disguised as a motion to the UN Security Council. New to office, both he and his advisers naïvely persisted with the belief that Serb and Croat aggression could be stalled if only the Muslims had better weapons. The thinly veiled American threat to support the UN move by Pakistan and Morocco, both Muslim countries, promised yet another round of transatlantic bickering. But, once again, the President had not bothered to do his homework.

The killing field of Bosnia was indeed desperately uneven. The Serb forces of about 150,000 regular and irregular troops had an estimated 300 tanks, 200 armoured personnel carriers and about 1000 artillery pieces, including howitzers, mortars, rocket launchers and recoilless rifles. The Muslims had only small arms and whatever they had managed to capture. At times they were reduced to sharing weapons and many a dead Muslim fighter was found without bullets in his rifle or spare magazines. One of their most lethal heavy weapons was a rubber tyre packed with explosives and nails, and rolled down the hill at Serb positions.

Offering to re-arm the Muslims was mindless White House magnanimity. It made no military sense and it was logistically impossible. Large numbers of spare weapons were available from ex-NATO stocks – M 60 and Leopard heavy tanks, light tanks and armoured personnel carriers, light and heavy field guns – and the war could only be made more equal if the Muslims were sent this kind of heavy weaponry. The Saudis and the Kuwaitis had promised to pay for them, but who would train the Muslims to use them and who would send the extra ground troops needed to protect the instructors? Not the Americans and not the Germans, even though both of them were pressing for the arms embargo to be lifted. The only countries with large numbers of troops committed in Bosnia were Britain and France and both those governments were opposed to arming the Muslims.

Even assuming that weapons could be bought, and the instructors and their protectors found, how would the tanks and artillery pieces be delivered? No Muslim-held land bordered the sea so they would have to go cross-country, and as all roads and railways went through either Serb or Croat territory, safe delivery could certainly not be guaranteed. Even if it was attempted, who would escort and protect such a massive, vulnerable, slow-moving convoy of heavy transporters from attack? Not the Americans, because they were opposed to committing troops on the ground and yet land supply was what they favoured. The only way to get the weapons to the Muslims was by air, but the only aircraft available to carry tanks and heavy artillery were the giant American Galaxies and there was not a runway anywhere in Bosnia long enough to take them.

Given these well-known and frequently quoted logistical impossibilities, it was surprising that President Clinton ever considered, let alone pursued the proposal. It was even more surprising that to overcome British and French opposition to it, he cunningly canvassed the support of the German President

Helmut Kohl, purposely bypassing the usual diplomatic channels.

However, much to the embarrassment of the White House and the Pentagon, the Anglo-French axis prevailed. The young President was obliged to retreat a second time with his tail between his legs and the Muslims went without.

In the final days of May, it was generally, if uneasily, accepted on both sides of the Atlantic that nothing could be done to reverse the Serbs' territorial gains, now over 70 per cent of Bosnia. The best that could be attempted was to contain the Serbs and persuade them and the Croats to agree to leave a tiny number of Muslim enclaves alone. Proudly announced as the Washington 'Joint Action Programme', when action was the last thing it promised, the surviving Muslims were told they could congregate in six 'Safe Havens': Sarajevo, Gorazde, Tuzla, Srebenica, Zepa and Bihac. At long last, and without even a blush, America, the UN and the European Community had given their *de facto* recognition of conquests made, agreeing in effect to let the conquerors redraw the Owen–Vance map using their own cartographers.

The Washington Agreement ended with the stern threat that the allies would regard any further extension of the conflict 'with the utmost seriousness' and would send 500 American military observers to the Macedonian border with Serbia to draw yet another line in the sand in the hope that Serb soldiers would not cross it. It was not likely to make the Serbs shudder. They had read the invisible ink. They could keep what they had but would they, please, leave a little bit for the Muslims? It was a victory for bluster, cowardice, dither and delay. Appeasement had won the day.

Like all those other plans drawn up by the advocates of doing nothing (and for two years now the British Foreign Secretary, Douglas Hurd, had been their most consistent champion), the havens began to collapse under a welter of Serb and Croat shells soon after the UN declared them safe. The UN did nothing. It said it would enlarge its peacekeeping force but it would still continue to operate under the same restricted rules of engagement, confined to the limited role of providing humanitarian assistance. They were not empowered to protect Muslim civilians from ethnic cleansing, sniper or shell. They could fire back to protect themselves, of course, and the snipers were reminded that they grazed a blue UN helmet at their peril. It was not so much a UN resolution for Bosnia as a UN plan for the UN. Asked if anything would be done to prevent the bombardment of villages within the safe havens, Mr Hurd replied: 'The agreement does not cover this.'

More than a million Muslims were now crowded into six besieged, isolated, unconnected ghettos, with the allies' approval and without their protection. They were tiny ink blots on the map, an archipelago in a hostile sea of Serbs. It was a last-ditch attempt to frustrate the Serbs and Croats from swallowing Bosnia whole and it was all that could be salvaged from the wreckage. The allies had hoped that the creation of safe havens was the formula for peace. They were disappointed: instead of the war coasting to a standstill it worsened in such a way that UN commanders on the ground were calling it by a new name. Anarchy.

The Serb and Croat High Commands had agreed to a cease-fire, but it seemed that their orders had not been received by the men behind the guns, who only intensified their shelling. In a new development, UN aid convoys were now being fired on and ambushed. Early in June, three Italian aid drivers were hauled from their lorries and shot dead by soldiers wearing Muslim cap badges belonging to the 317 Brigade, whose commander was the flamboyant Hanefija Paraga. He wore a hat with the British Desert Rat insignia on it and his bodyguard was a blond carrying a Kalishnikov automatic rifle. The following day two Danish drivers and their interpreter were killed in a Serb ambush while they were trying to take food and medicines to Maglaj in central Bosnia where, local radio reports said, the main street was littered with human limbs.

Because of these and other attacks on roads leading to

Muslim areas, aid workers were now able to deliver less than half what was desperately needed and even those convoys that had armed escorts were being attacked by all three sides. Total UN casualties, military and civilian, now topped 500, including forty-three dead. The UN sent a letter of warning to its aid workers reminding them that: 'Safe areas have been declared but are not being protected. Areas that should be safe are not. Killing and ethnic cleansing continues unabated.'

Muslim gunmen ambushed a British patrol and stripped them of weapons and equipment. British troops were fired on and returned fire when a 500-vehicle Muslim evacuation convoy that they were protecting – it was called the 'Convoy of Joy' – was attacked by Croat gunmen near to the British base at Vitez. After the Croats had pulled Muslim drivers from their cabs and shot eight of them dead, the crew of a British Warrior armoured car opened fire with their machine-gun and killed two of the Croat gunmen.

A few days later, as if to illustrate the murderous idiocy of the war, the same British troops rescued 200 Croat civilians under fire from Muslim militiamen. Seven Croats were killed, and as they were buried, the British army chaplain had to shout the Lord's Prayer to be heard above the din of the firing.

The Cheshires who had made up most of the 2,500 strong British UN contingent at Vitez were about to be replaced by the Prince of Wales' Own Regiment of Yorkshire. The Cheshires' last month of duty was their bloodiest by far. Having spent their tour helping to evacuate refugees and escort aid convoys into enclaves under siege, they, too, suddenly found themselves encircled as Muslims and Croats fought each other in the surrounding towns and villages. Soon they were calling it the Valley of Death.

With the world's attention focused on the Serb onslaught against the Muslims in the east and their renewed offensive on Gorazde, one of the UN's safe havens, the Croats had revived their own campaign of ethnic cleansing and land-grabbing in central Bosnia in and around Mostar and Travnik. The Muslims, who had once considered the Croats their allies in the fight against the Serbs, now found themselves at war with them. Some of the bloodiest fighting was in the ethnically mixed area around Vitez and the small town of Kiseljak, close to Sarajevo. In the first two days, over 200 people, Muslims and Croats were killed. Seven hundred were to die before the fighting ended six weeks later.

The cold-blooded executions committed by both sides shocked the young British soldiers who had seen nothing like it before – nor had they ever expected to. Families were shot, hanged, decapitated, disembowelled, lined up against a wall and their throats cut, locked inside their homes and burned alive. The soldiers found more than ninety bodies in the tiny Muslim village of Ahmici – old people, women and children, who had been left behind unprotected as their men were away fighting. Most were unrecognizable as people. Some had been blasted to pieces, others had been locked in their cellars which had been set on fire. What the men of the Cheshires scooped out of the mud and cinders that day was described by one soldier, a boy of nineteen as, 'strips of meat and twisted sticks of charcoal'. The soldiers' own sense of tragedy was heightened by having been close to the village only hours before and having thought the area safe.

The Cheshires were heroes in one other episode which provided them with much-needed relief and has been recorded in their regimental log as one of their finest hours. It concerned the rescue of a brown bear they had nicknamed Big Mac, after General Lewis Mackenzie, the popular one-time UN commander in Sarajevo. Big Mac was trapped inside a cage close to the British base and had narrowly escaped being shot dead by snipers. Having negotiated a temporary ceasefire with both the Croat and Muslim local commanders, the Cheshires coaxed Big Mac out of his cage with honey-coated apples and into a waiting army lorry. Then, with an escort of two Warriors, he was driven down to Split on the Dalmatian coast where he expects to spend the rest of his retirement.

More and more frequently, the blue United Nations' flag and the Union Jack that fluttered above the British base in Vitez and on every British army vehicle were being fired at. One British soldier had already been killed and there were fears that, in the anarchy that now reigned, the British, having killed once, would soon have to kill again. They had been sucked in to do what the UN mandate forbade them; protect those who could not protect themselves and every day the risk increased. There were angry demands in Parliament for them to be withdrawn and hints by ministers that, if things got worse, the troops would indeed be evacuated. In the Adriatic, the Royal Navy's aircraft carrier *Ark Royal* steamed a little closer to the Dalmatian port of Split and her captain, Terence Loughran, began to review the logistics for a helicopter land-to-sea shuttle. In Sarajevo, after French legionnaires were hit by Serb fire as they defended the airport, the UN commander, General Philippe Morillon, announced that if attacks against UN personnel continued, 'We will, with rage and sadness in our hearts, have no option but withdraw.'

Which was, of course, exactly what the Serbs had in mind. They quickly gave the General their reply that same evening with the heaviest bombardment of the city in more than a month. Shells hit his own headquarters and, for the first time, his residence. In the twenty-four hours of bombardment, twenty people were killed, twelve of them at a football game in the Muslim suburb of Dobrinja. One hundred and seventy were wounded.

The following day, the people of Sarajevo held a beauty contest. Those who knew the city well did not think it bizarre, even after fourteen months of siege. Had they not already sent six contestants scrambling through the ruins to sing their 'Song of Freedom' at the Eurovision Song Contest in Ireland? And had not one of them been shot dead in the escape? Now the prettiest girls of a city once famous for its chic paraded in front of the judges, one of them a general with an AK 47 assault rifle in his lap, to compete for the title 'Miss Besieged Sarajevo'. As the thirteen contestants in their leotards and swimsuits swung their hips along the catwalk, the loudspeakers blared out the hit song 'Eve of Destruction'. A mile away, the hospital admitted over eighty casualties while twenty-two new corpses were laid out in the morgue.

Bosko Brckic was a twenty-five-year-old chemistry student. For seven years he had dated the same girl, Admira Ismic, a student in his class. They had been sweethearts since school, and once the war was over they were going to be married. Bosko was a Serb and Admira a Muslim but in Sarajevo such a courtship was not unusual. Once it had been Bosnia's proud symbol of tolerance.

Bosko's widowed mother and brother had fled to Serbia when the war began but he stayed behind because Admira could not leave. Muslims were the victims of the siege and for her there was no escape. Until Bosko told her his plan. He had paid the local Muslim commander to allow them a safe passage out of the city by a secret route across the Miljacka river. She agreed to take the risk and, early that Wednesday evening, she packed their things into a small carrier bag and made the rendezvous just before dusk. Nervously, hand in hand, they crossed the Vrbanja bridge. The hump, where the two arches joined, was no man's land, a yard or so of tarmac that separated other Serbs and Muslims but for these two, boy and girl, it was their window to freedom.

The sniper's first bullet hit Bosko in the neck and killed him instantly. Admira turned to go back as the second hit her. Slowly, and knowing her life was draining away, she pulled herself towards him, wrapped her arms around him in a final embrace and then died with her hair covering his face. For five days they left the bodies on Vrbanja bridge. Neither Serb nor Muslim would let the other take them to be buried. Nor would they let the UN soldiers carry them decently away. For those five days, the lovers lay together in their embrace, reminding all who dared to look, Serb and Muslim, that two young Bosnians had died not from hate but from their love. On the sixth day, they came for the bodies. The Serbs took Bosko. The Muslims took Admira.

Finally, they were separated.

Bosnia was dead but the burial would take some time. There were still claimants to the corpse. There were still those who believed in miracles and thought it could be resurrected. The Vance–Owen peace plan had at last been consigned to the waste-bin and in its place, foreign ministers and warmongers alike were about to agree the partition of Bosnia into three. Gone was the meticulously crafted ethnic jigsaw of confederation that the peacebrokers had so patiently hawked around the world's chancellories. Gone was the make-believe map, the patchwork quilt of Owen optimism, where the warring tribes who had spent the past two years raping each other's wives and murdering each other's children were supposed to live in good faith and neighbourliness under the benevolent custody of a massive UN army of peace-enforcers.

The men behind the orgy of ethnic butchery were finishing what they began and with far more reward than they ever expected. There was jubilation in the capitals of Serbia and Croatia. Wounds were licked. Soon they would be healed and forgotten. Serbia's President Milosevic, the man who more than any other had conceived the war and ensured the Serbian victory, was now being publicly praised by Lord Owen for 'his good offices in the search for peace'. Douglas Hurd endorsed the sentiment and, as for condemning Milosevic as a war criminal, as he had been indicted only a few months before, Mr Hurd thought it, 'A little excessive to use that kind of language in the circumstances.' American and European leaders readily accepted Bosnia's death and the brutal reality of a Serb victory, and prayed that the Muslims would stop resisting and accept the carve-up like good losers. Then the television crews would go home, the carnage would be off the screens and ministers and presidents could get on with the more pertinent, career-threatening problems of political scandals, health reforms and recurrent recessions. The caring public had also grown weary. The daily diet of death and destruction had finally made Bosnia yet another casualty of compassion fatigue: the horrors and atrocities that had once mesmerized the world had become too commonplace to stir the conscience any more.

The knock-on to that was donor fatigue. It meant that international aid and cash being offered to the UN and other non-government aid agencies suddenly dropped to less than a quarter of what it had been. Overnight, the sick and the hungry of Bosnia would get less than a quarter of what it was estimated they needed to survive.

June was the month in which the tide of war turned and midsummer day was just about its watershed. From then on, the frenetic peacebroking and public anxiety began to drain away. It was time to close the file on the Balkans. Almost overnight it seemed, the warmongers had become the peacemakers and everyone persuaded themselves that a little peace in Bosnia was better than none at all. Any serious territorial concessions to the Muslims were now out of the question.

The world outside consoled itself that it had been sympathetic, but sympathy had not been enough to stop the killing. The world had sent dried milk and bandages but it had put its blind eye to the telescope as the Serbs and Croats slaughtered and stole land unchallenged. The international community had hidden behind diplomatic code words and stumbled through two years of wishful thinking, but it had not been prepared to defend the principles it had long proclaimed as its foundations. They were no longer valid. After more than a year of wringing their hands over Bosnia, the allies were about to wash them. It was their penultimate move in the Judas game.

At a secret meeting in the Montenegrin coastal town of Hercog Novi, the Bosnian-Serb leader, Dr Radavan Karadzic, and his Bosnian-Croat counterpart, Mate Boban, mapped out those parts of Bosnia they would keep as their own as well as those parts they hoped might be negotiable and exchanged at a later date. The Serbs' main territorial concern was to widen the northern corridor linking their western possessions to their eastern ones and thus to Serbia itself. The Croats had consolidated land to the north and north-west. Both sides agreed to help each other destroy the last isolated pockets of Muslim resistance such as Mostar and Maglaj in central and eastern Bosnia. The days when Serb and Croat viewed each other through the sights of a gun were over. At least, that was what was being said.

As part of the new *entente cordiale*, they agreed it was crucial to a settlement for the future also to be discussed. Much Croat territory was still held by the Serbs, including Vukovar and the thorn-in-the-side Krijina. With a bigger and better army, Dr Karadzic feared the Croats might one day want to retake lost lands in a far more sophisticated war of tanks and missiles and jet fighter-bombers. He knew, because it had just been published in Jane's *Sentinel*, a British defence information service, that the Croats had bought nearly one billion pounds' worth of heavy weapons over the past eighteen months.

In subsequent meetings in the Croatian capital Zagreb and then Geneva, Serb and Croat leaders endorsed the partition. Bosnia, like Caesar's Gaul, would be split three ways: the Serbs, who represented about a third of the population in pre-war Bosnia, would have nearly three-quarters of the land (the Owen–Vance map had offered them less than half); the Croats, who made up 17 per cent, would get about a fifth; and the Muslims, the majority, would be lucky to get the remaining improper fraction.

The arithmetic of betrayal was governed by the common denominator of conquest, and the Muslim leader, Alija Izet-begovic, walked out of the initial meetings, refusing even to discuss partition. Not that it mattered, he was head of a state that no longer existed. There was no room for protest now. The Muslims had to be content with little or nothing at all.

They were to be consigned to their six disjointed havens and half of what was left of the battered Sarajevo. The Serbs had unilaterally declared they would keep all of the city south of the Miljacka river. To many this would be the foulest crime of all: despite its ethnic mix, Sarajevo had never been divided. On the map the river might look like a convenient dividing line but it made no more sense than splitting London along the Thames. Unlike so many cities in the world, the people of Sarajevo were cosmopolitan and had never congregated in ghettos and districts. There were no Muslim, Serb, Croat or Jewish quarters – that was what they had been most proud of.

When the partition of Sarajevo was announced, journalists in the city reported a terrible melancholy. Its people had lived fifteen months under siege, ten thousand at least had died gruesome deaths, many thousands more had suffered the most horrible injuries. The rest had survived against all the odds and yet in the end it meant nothing. That day the American correspondent Charles Glass wrote:

> . . . the shells were falling particularly heavily and a woman
> followed me down the stairs to a safe seat by a solid wall.
> She lit a cigarette and began to sing, probably to calm
> herself. Her voice was haunting. I asked her what the words
> meant and she translated: 'All the sadness of the world is
> mine tonight.'

Once, the Muslims had been the majority in Bosnia but now they would exist on sufferance, trusting the UN to continue to feed them, possessing not even a contiguous strip of territory, dependent on the cooperation and goodwill of the Serbs or Croats surrounding them. The war had taught them something new about Serbs, Croats and goodwill. Partition three ways would generate the biggest movement of people seen in Europe this century as Muslims fled to their designated areas and Serbs and Croats took up the land they left. The exodus would resemble the flight of Muslims to Pakistan and Hindus to India after the British Raj left the subcontinent.

The British Foreign Secretary Douglas Hurd had once vehemently and publicly declared that Bosnia would never be partioned. Now he conceded, 'This is best we can hope for.' But it was not the best *they* had hoped for, the millions of Muslims who had become outcasts in their own country. By accepting the Serb-Croat agenda for peace, America and its allies had recognized 'separate development' and in so doing the rebirth of ethnic supremacy at Europe's centre. A new apartheid had been condoned, born of butchers and bigotry.

As July became August, it appeared to be all over bar the crying. Bosnia lay dying and the inheritors came to Geneva to finish the task of dismembering it limb by limb. A year ago, western leaders at the London Conference under the British Prime Minister's chairmanship, hailed as another of his triumphs, had solemnly pledged to: 'Uphold the sovereign integrity of Bosnia, to end Serb aggression and to reverse ethnic cleansing'. Now these same leaders and the same Prime Minister, had given their tacit assent to Bosnia's division into three.

At the hugely expensive white marble United Nation's palace by Lake Geneva, once the home of the impotent and disgraced League of Nations, the Muslim Bosnian leader President Alija Izetbegovic was about to surrender. That Sunday evening, the first day of August, sitting in his Geneva hotel, (suitably called The President), he prepared to broadcast a message to his people via Radio Sarajevo. The wingback armchair dwarfed him. A little man, he seemed to shrink visibly with every new capitulation, as if he lost flesh with every extra bit of lost territory. He broadcast without a script; what he had to say was not long and he had had the opportunity to rehearse it a dozen times over during the past few months. 'Partition', he said, 'is the only option to suicide. We will not survive another winter. We have no choice.' Midway, he paused to wipe away his tears. His listeners would not have known he was weeping but they did hear loud explosions in the background and screaming noises they thought they recognized as incoming shells. They might have wondered whether Geneva, the very nucleus of world peace, was itself under attack. But outside in the streets along the edge of their famously beautiful lake, the Swiss were celebrating their National Day and the fireworks and coloured rockets provided the sad little President with a bizarre background as he ended his country's epitaph.

How jubilant the Serbs were. How they strutted in front of the world's Press, the victorious President Milosevic and his subservient sibling Dr Karadzic. 'We have a peace and we are satisfied,' said the President with a smile. 'No one else now need die over Bosnia, there is nothing more to gain,' echoed the doctor, adding to his litany of lies. Yet how familiar it all was to those of us who witnessed it, such overwhelming déjàs vu. And how suddenly it was finished, how abruptly, almost neatly. Surely, we thought, there must be another page to the transcript? And there was.

The Serbs appeared to have got what they wanted in one week's intensive negotiation. So confident were they, they had even brought their own map and Lord Owen had given it his nod of approval. But no sooner had they left for their separate homes in their separate executive jets when the one Serb who had not been in Geneva and who should have been if the outcome was to have any meaning, had decided on another route to victory. Even as the politicians had been talking, General Ratko MLadic, the Serb Napoleon, was marching up Mount Igman overlooking Sarajevo to push the last of the Muslim fighters off it. Hardly a shot had been fired but now the Serbs were in control of the most strategically important mountain, because from it they controlled all the routes that supplied the city and its forces with food and ammunition. Once again, the manic MLadic had stymied both his enemy and his own political masters and by that second August Sunday, he stood with his army commanders, flanked by his tanks and artillery, with the city he had held siege for sixteen months sprawled beneath him and at his mercy.

Maybe the drama of it finally touched the soul of President

Clinton. Suddenly, he was belicose, pounding the drum, sounding the alarm, raising his voice. Perhaps, as his cruellest critics suggested, he needed some foreign diversion to take America's mind off his domestic tassle with Congress over the Budget deficit. Maybe he was playing to the oil sheikhs, the Saudis and the Kuwaitis, who felt they ought to help their Muslim brothers if only from distant sidelines. More likely, Bosnia had now shrunk so small it was a size the President could more easily comprehend, one that fitted the limited attention he could divert to it.

Whatever the reason, with the Serb guns ready to pound the very gates of Sarajevo and after so many months of acting like a sheep in wolf's clothing, the President began talking of air strikes . . . again! The White House media management brigade went at their task full pelt, bombarding the world's press with evidence of Presidential outrage. He would not allow the Serb strangulation of Sarajevo to continue one day longer, the noose would not be tightened and he would immediately confer with his NATO allies and win their agreement to air strikes so as to ensure the survival of a Bosnian Muslim state. To many who listened to the White House announcements it was as if, like Snow White, the President had just awakened from a long, long sleep!

But as always, saying did not make it so. He was faced with the same dilemma as before. Two of his allies, Britain and France, were still less than keen on air strikes. They had between them around six thousand soldiers on the ground in Bosnia and it was not at all certain how easily they might be retrieved whole when the Serbs retaliated, as they most certainly would. What would happen to the supply of humanitarian aid then? British military advisers also pointed out that American strategy was flawed. Hitting Serb positions might cause them some disruption and a few casualties but armies do not surrender to aircraft and if the power equation was not radically changed on the ground, and unless the US or the UN were prepared to follow up with a rapid massive deployment of ground troops, not a lot would be accomplished.

The President had also to impress upon the Bosnian Muslims that American-led air attacks on Serb positions on Mount Igman did not imply the US Seventh Cavalry was on the other side of it ready to canter to their rescue. In short, that American military intervention on the Muslim side to turn the tide of war was not, and never would be, an option. But American denials fell on deaf Muslim ears. As soon as the threat of air strikes was announced, President Izetbegovic stalled. Suddenly, he found things to object to, like the lines on the map that only days before he had accepted as inevitable and final. The negotiations went backwards and Lord Owen was furious, singling out Reginald Bartholomew, President Clinton's man on the ground in Geneva and blaming him and his master for undoing what it had taken so long to put together.

Mr Clinton had wrong-footed it again. Perhaps he was getting wrong advice. Or ignoring good. Most certainly, his own well-publicized moral conflict risked landing the West in a military quagmire. Those who knew the map of Bosnia well and the character of the Serbs better, reckoned the tactic was wrong on every level and merely compounded the West's disarray. America's own excuse of a Balkan policy looked ever more infantile. Only the Serbs, it seemed, had scored. So for another fortnight, the politicians and the generals anguished over the rights and wrongs of air attacks and whether they would ever have the courage to order them. Meanwhile, American and British pilots dipped their fighter-bombers in and out of the white clouds in practice sorties above Sarajevo, checking Serb gun and tank positions on Mount Igman and relaying their information back to the planners at their base at Vicenza in Italy. And a hundred forward air controllers, the men who would sit on the ground and direct the laser-guided bombs to their targets, began to arrive in the Dalmatian port of Split, waiting for the order to disperse to secret destinations throughout Bosnia.

As if to divert attention from the mess it was in, now made suddenly all the more dangerous by the prospect of Mr Clinton's hit-and-run air strikes, the UN in Sarajevo unveiled OPER-

ATION LIFELINE. It was simply its old mandate dressed up but with the added rider that it was now dependent on the Serb's pledge to leave the UN's supply routes into the city open. It quickly became known as Operation Loophole because if the Serbs did that, it would take away the need for air strikes. The UN had unwittingly offered the Serbs the advantage and they saw how they could use it as their *coup de grâce*. Commanding the supply routes would ensure that only food and medicines entered the city, so that the Muslim fighters inside it would thereafter be denied weapons and ammunition. On their commander's own admission Sarajevo would soon be forced to surrender. So the Serbs had only to play the endgame with their familiar ruthless cunning and they might have the final prize before the autumn. Then, at last, the negotiators could empty their maps and protocols and draft resolutions into the diplomatic dustbin. There would be nothing to talk about any more.

As I write these closing pages it is late summer and the Serbs would seem to be attempting exactly that. But this war has had many tragic turns and by the time you read this you will already know its new course. To many, perhaps most, it has been a bewildering war and bloodier than any would ever had thought possible. But there never was any uncertainty who would be the winner, only how many people would be lost in the winning of it.

There was seldom any doubt, among those of us who reported it, how it could be resolved and brought to an end quickly and we were never short on advice. But it needed resolution, courage, the rare ability to be decisive and responsive to demands beyond and above personal and national self interests. Our politicians, we cannot comfortably call them leaders, failed on all counts, too consumed were they with treacherous rhetoric. Britain's own Foreign Secretary, Douglas Hurd, was the champion of Do-Nothing Diplomacy and like donkeys, he led the rest. Despite his sometimes solemn, sometimes jaunty façade, the fictional short stories he has written about Bosnia this past year, has revealed the guilt he feels about the slaughter he would not stop there. The list of others who should share his torment is too long to mention.

A year ago I made a solemn promise to take Natasha back to Bosnia by the time the new school term began or when the war ended, whichever was sooner. I have the piece of paper still, a pledge with my signature on it, rubber-stamped and official. The war is now ending, at least for a while, and perhaps before the year is over the schools might unlock their doors again, wherever schools are still standing.

But I will not keep that promise. So many, anyway, have been broken over Bosnia that my little one will go unnoticed. It will be some time before the survivors there, once they are out of their cellars and into their safe havens, clear the debris of war and begin to resurrect something of the old order. Demands for the return of those who managed to run away will be low on their priority list.

I shall have broken my word to Vera Zoric but, if she is still alive, she will know why. The war had only just begun when we made our agreement that evening in the orphanage, to the sound of exploding shells and mortars, and she could not have known what was to come. Who did, then? Who could have imagined how long the war would last or how it would be fought with a ferocity and savagery barely believable?

Long before her first anniversary, Natasha had pushed away the ghosts of Sarajevo's yesteryears that, in the beginning, had haunted and taunted her. The uncertainties are dimming and hopefully, soon, they will be all but extinguished. She has become absorbed into English ways among English people and so immersed is she now in her England that Bosnia has become like a distant landscape, barely visible. There is a saying that the things we remember best are those better forgotten and much of her year has seen her filtering out those bits of her past she needs to forget.

She misses her friends still but they are now happily scattered across new homes in Italy and Germany, Denmark and Sweden and, like her other memories, their faces and names are fading fast. People who mean well have criticized us for tearing her away from what was hers, denying her the community she was born into and the heritage that was her birthright. We have, it seems to some, performed an unkind cultural lobotomy.

History is our defence and explanation. Where is her community now? What remains of her heritage? What would Natasha return to? An orphanage, a shell-shaken ruin in a shell-shocked half of a city, a Croat in a ghetto of imprisoned Muslims? Would she live among other Croats, strangers all and alien, or with her aunt and uncle who, for nine years, knew of their little niece in the Sarajevo orphanage but did not offer her their home or their family?

I brought her into our care and together Diana and I have done it our way. We saturated her with ourselves, with our kind of living. We surrounded her with our home, our family and friends, the house, the village, the school, roast beef and Yorkshire pud, Brownies, fêtes, singing with the 'Jesus Team', her dancing lessons, cricket, football, netball, camping by the fire, holidays by the sea, our bad moods and our good times, our discipline and occasional lack of it. None of it was done hesitantly or with anyone's say-so. We did not constantly remind her of who she was or where she came from or why she was here.

The do-gooders cautioned us and told us we were being too ambitious, even irresponsible and that such a complete break with her past would be traumatic and do her lasting psychological damage. We were advised that she would need counselling and therapy and would almost certainly need the regular company of her own people to speak her own language and be reminded she was a Slav.

That was not our way. It was quite enough for her to cope with one thing at a time at her own pace: learning a new language, meeting new people and making new friends. She had to discover the strange geography of a new home in a new town in a new country.

It was also her way. She had been brought up to be a survivor and she quickly recognized that her real task was not to maintain her differentness but to adapt, to be absorbed, to imprint herself, to make Natasha seem less foreign.

There is no going back for us now. It is a matter of 'for better or worse'. We are usually given only one chance in life to change it and if, on that day in Sarajevo, I could not know what would happen when I changed it so suddenly for her, I could guess what would happen if I did not.

It was a gamble then and we know – and she must herself – that it will remain one for a long, long time yet.

Natasha will not go back. Perhaps one day, she tells me, when she is a big girl, we will all return to see what had been her country, the land that once upon a time was called Bosnia, where, it is written in the history books, people lived contentedly together, married one another, whose children played together, Serb and Croat and Muslim, side by side, village by village, blissfully unaware of the fuse that, smouldering slowly and imperceptibly for centuries, finally ignited a holocaust.